STAGE EFFECTS AND PROPS
FOR EASTER AND CHRISTMAS

A Lillenas DRAMA TOPICS SERIES

STAGE EFFECTS AND PROPS FOR EASTER AND CHRISTMAS

Written and Illustrated
by Lee Eric Shackleford

Lillenas PUBLISHING COMPANY

KANSAS CITY, MO 64141

For
Bernard Block
one of two Jewish miracle-workers
who have taught me,
sustained me,
and given me hope.

Some Personal Words

I am deeply indebted to Paul Miller
for the opportunity to set some of these bizarre ideas
on paper,
and to my wife, Kinta Parker,
for her unfailing support during the somewhat crazed
period in which this book was written,
and to my parents,
who did not judge me as "abnormal"
when I took my toys apart
and built new ones out of the pieces,
but most of all
to the Creator of All Things
in the hope that whenever any of us rejoices
at having built something that works
the way it is supposed to,
we have some inkling how He feels
when we do His will
the way we are supposed to.

Contents

Introduction

The Greatest Story Ever Told

This book assumes that you're preparing the production of a drama based on the Life of Christ. If you are, then no matter what kind of performing group you have—large or small, experienced or novice, rich or poor, young or mature—you are venturing into difficult territory.

Part of the challenge that awaits you is in the simple fact that you're depicting the spectacular events of the Christ story. To begin with, Judea of the first century was a complex and dangerous place—volcanically violent, rough-edged, and rugged. And into this arena came the Messiah, the promised Son of God. He made this exciting, long-ago world an even more astounding place to live. Angels heralded His arrival. He turned ordinary water into perfect wine. He took a couple of pieces of bread and a few fish and fed a multitude. He was brutally murdered . . . then returned from the dead and was taken up into heaven.

And this is what you're expected to show onstage.

Fortunately, these are the obstacles this book can help you overcome. But before we start tackling these problems, let's consider another, more important part of the challenge that is now confronting you. That is the story itself.

As you know, it's no ordinary tale. It's what novelist Fulton Oursler called "The Greatest Story Ever Told." It's the epic of how the Son of God lived on earth so that we might learn how He wants us to live—and of how He died and rose again to free us from the burden of our own sins. It's the saga of the pivotal moment in all human history.

And this is also what you're expected to show onstage.

Fear not! You are blessed. I believe God smiles on you and on your production just because *you want to tell the story.* You are preaching the gospel when you present your Christmas pageant, your passion play, or your Easter drama. You preach the gospel as surely as your minister/priest/pastor/preacher does from behind the pulpit. And that, my friends, will bless you and your audience alike. You undertake this project with God on your side.

Much of what I've just said is probably obvious to you. But I remind you of it for a very important reason. There is a powerful temptation for people staging a Christian drama to concentrate on "getting the presentation right" at the expense of the message to be presented. We've all seen it time and again: an awesome spectacle of a passion play, an impressively designed Easter pageant, a charming or adorable Christmas show . . . that didn't teach the audience about the Story. And while the book you're reading now is designed to help you make the best-*looking*, best-*sounding* presentation you can, all of us here at Lillenas pray you will not let these "tricks of the trade" steal the show.

Avoiding this pitfall will require prayerful, well-considered judgment on the part of your director, designers, craftsmen, and performers.

Let me offer an example.

In one passion play for which I was an effects designer, the other designers and I figured out how to make a flail with which the actor portraying Jesus could be "scourged" without actually doing him injury.

It made a horrific (and appropriate) noise and left painful-looking stripes on his back. A very impressive effect. The audience was filled with awe at our technical prowess—but *not* at the silent Jesus enduring this torture. For many people in the audience, the suffering of our Lord was no longer the point of the scene. The special effect took the spotlight—and actually upstaged Jesus Christ (or at least, our presentation of Him).

We had already rejected the solution of having our Jesus facing downstage while the jailer cracked the whip behind him, well upstage of him. But later we realized that this effect would have been simpler, easier, less show-offy—and

would have *kept the face of the Christ where the audience could see it!* Instead we got carried away with the challenge of realistic special effects.

I believe that if our design team had discussed this part of the show beforehand, we would have seen that we were focusing on a *stunt* and not on the *story*—making Jesus less important than our showing off.

So I encourage you to have a special planning meeting on this very subject. Get all of your people together in a quiet place, pray for guidance, and open the floor to discussion of how the play can best be used to teach the gospel message. Consider the costumes, the lighting, the props, and the special effects. Ask yourself who is glorified by each of these things. Is the purpose of this show to demonstrate the resources of your congregation? Or the cleverness of your cast and crew? Or is this a sincere attempt to tell the Story?

Then I believe you will see something wonderful happen, something I've seen happen time after time: you'll see genuine miracles happening in your production.

And I believe you will then see miracles happening in your audience.

—Lee Eric Shackleford

Part One
Special Effects

Since some readers of this book are preparing Christmas shows while others are looking ahead to Easter, let's assume that we are going to stage a telling of the entire life of Christ. This way we will cover all the material you are liable to encounter in any canonical telling of the story.[1]

Let us begin, then, at the beginning.

Angels

Whether you are following Matthew's Nativity narrative or Luke's, you're going to need to show Mary, Joseph, and the infant Jesus. Easy so far[2]—but then come the "messengers and the celestial host." They present challenges for even the most professional and well-equipped theatrical setting.

What Should Your Angels Look Like?

The Bible tells us relatively little about the first angels in the New Testament; only that it is Gabriel who brings the good news to Mary,[3] and it's an unnamed angel in a dream who visits Joseph.[4] We are not told if they fly, if they glow, if they have wings or halos, or if they look like cherubs, Greek gods, or ghosts. We are simply told that they visited Mary and Joseph, spoke to them, and "departed."

So this offers a wide degree of latitude. While the tradition of angels as winged beings floating in the sky is a powerful one, there is in fact nothing in Scripture to require that Mary and Joseph's angels flew. So if your script calls for either one or both of these heavenly messengers, you may simply have them enter the stage as any other character would.

Apparel like Lightning

If you are of the opinion that angels must at least have radiant appearances,[5] make sure that your lighting design allows for them to be brilliantly illuminated with a tight enough beam to keep everyone else onstage in relative darkness. This is also a case where working closely with your scenic artists and costumers will also serve you well; you may try dressing Mary and Joseph in dark, matte natural tones (rust, deep green, etc.) and making sure that props and scenery nearby are also muted and dark in color. Then introduce the angel, dressed in purest white with focused lighting aimed right at his or her torso. The costume will virtually fluoresce in contrast to everything else.

For an even more striking effect, you may want to invest in a miraculous-seeming material made by the 3M Corporation, trademarked as ScotchLite. Basically a variation on the super-reflective paint used on many road signs, ScotchLite is available in various forms, such as plastic sheeting, adhesive tape, and fabric. The substance reflects almost 100% of any light that strikes it—much more than almost anything found in nature. Dressing angels in this fabric will indeed cause them to appear "like lightning."[6]

Incidentally, if your production calls for you to show the Transfigura-

1. This book assumes throughout that your intention is to present a tale of the Christ that is as accurate as possible according to the Canon; that is, to the four Gospels. You may find that there are few things more embarrassing in church drama than creating a prop or effect that seems to work perfectly—and then realizing that the end product contradicts Scripture. So I encourage you to begin your work on the props and effects for this show with a careful, line-by-line comparison of your script with the canonical Gospels. For this purpose I recommend the United Bible Societies' *Synopsis of the Four Gospels,* available at your local Christian bookseller.

2. That is, it will be easy if you resist the temptation to use a live baby as the Blessed Infant. I have never seen a production with a real infant that did not (*a*) terrify the child and (*b*) include a presentation of "Silent Night" throughout which the baby howled at the top of his lungs.

3. In Luke 1:26-38.

4. In Matthew 1:18-21, and again in Matthew 2:13, then yet again in Matthew 2:19-20.

5. Some biblical encounters with angels refer to their being "dazzling," often "like lightning"—as in Matthew 28:2-3, to name only one example.

6. For a very striking example of ScotchLite fabric at work, see the opening sequences of the 1978 film *Superman.* Marlon Brando and Susannah York are dressed in this fabric and carefully lit so most of the light bounces straight back into the camera—it's a remarkable effect. See the Appendix for sources of ScotchLite.

7. That is, the events described in Matthew 17, Mark 9, and most fully in Luke 9:28-36. Note that in all three accounts special mention is made of the dazzling brilliance of Jesus' clothes.

tion[7] onstage, you may want to consider somehow using ScotchLite in the costumes for Jesus, Moses, and Elijah.

One Option: Keeping Your Angels on the Ground

Can you do justice to the second chapter of the Gospel of Luke without dealing with flying angels? Maybe so. Even in that passage of Scripture that deals with the shepherds abiding in the fields, Luke does *not* expressly state that the angels and the "heavenly host" appear in the sky—only that they appear.

So the very practical tradition of using the church's choir as the "heavenly host" may serve you well. In hundreds of Christmas pageants all over the world, Luke 2 is enacted with the robed choir entering the stage and standing on risers to sing "Joy to the World." And this is a stylistic choice as much as anything: in your Nativity drama this may be all that is needed to remind the audience of the celestial singers that so amazed those shepherds keeping watch over their flocks by night.

Another Option: Putting Your Angels in the Air

But according to Luke, these angels do "disappear into heaven," presumably rising into the sky if they weren't there already. And centuries of religious art (and decades of Christmas cards) have taught us that the angels appear in the sky singing and praising God, so this is something your audience may expect. Let's assume that you are going to attempt to show this in your Christmas pageant.

One simple method is to put the angels on scaffolding or tall platforms that have been draped in a cloth that matches the background. This is a solution that works on almost any budget, and if properly lit can be quite effective. The main trick is in keeping the structures well-balanced enough to be safe. The completed assembly must still provide easy enough access from the upstage [back] side that your performers can get up to the perch—in the dark!

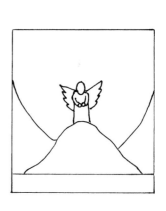

Many passion plays use variations on this effect for their angels, leaving the structure onstage throughout so the actor playing Jesus can use it for the Ascension. The visual impact of beginning and ending the presentation with the same effect can be very powerful; we know that Jesus is going up into heaven because He is up where the angels were.

Using Scrim for a Dramatic Revelation

A more complex variation on this involves the use of scenic scrim, a wonderful fabric that appears opaque when lit from the front but translucent when lit from behind.[8] If your performance space permits it, the scrim would be hung like this:

8. See the Appendix for sources on scrim and other materials.

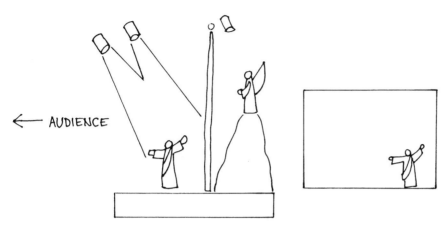

Most scenes in the drama would be lit from the downstage side of the scrim, rendering the area upstage of the scrim invisible. For scenes involving the angels, the vast majority of the lighting would come from upstage of the scrim, revealing the angels on their perches. Another advantage of this method is that the scrim diffuses the light that reflects back to the audience, so very little of the unlit areas upstage would be visible.

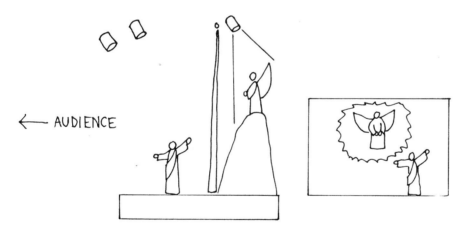

If you're able to make use of this effect, you may find it has all sorts of advantages. The Transfiguration, for example, could be presented in the same way as the angels and the Ascension. It could also be used for instant scene changes—for example, if you want to show Jesus on trial before the Sanhedrin at the same time that Peter denies Him,[9] the courtyard could be represented by the downstage area and the meeting room of the Sanhedrin council could be shown upstage. With a single lighting cue, the scene could shift from one to the other. Much simpler than moving furniture on and off the stage!

9. As in John 18:12-27, for example.

"Really" Flying an Angel

Let's assume for a moment that you have the budget, facility, and inclination to show angels actually flying through the air. It can be done—as anyone who has seen the Christmas pageant at the famous Crystal Cathedral in Garden Grove, California, can attest.

This is accomplished with a "flying rig," a complex structure that includes a harnesslike device worn by a performer and strong but thin wires that are attached to the harness at one end and to a scaffolding at the other from which the "flying" person is essentially controlled like a marionette.

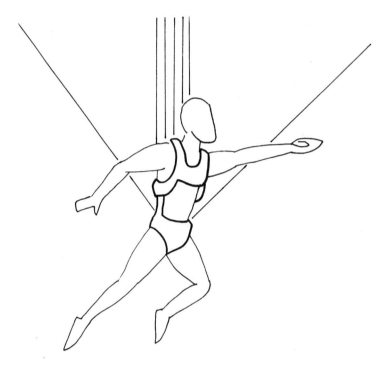

(This is not an accurate drawing of the rig, just an attempt to show you the general idea. Besides, if I showed exactly how the rig works, someone might attempt to duplicate it—and I don't want the inevitable accident to happen to them.)

Getting all of this machinery up into the air involves a structural analysis of the building where this stunt will be performed, and the installation of heavy equipment into the ceiling and walls. It is even more difficult than making the actor fly, but many would say the final effect is worth all the effort.[10]

Stars

If you're telling the Christmas story according to Matthew, your next big special effects challenge will probably arise in the form of a miraculous star to be followed by the magi.[11] You may feel you need other stars as well. Let's take these problems one at a time, beginning with the magi's star, or the star over the City of David.

The Star of Bethlehem

I have seen utterly charming Christmas pageants in which the star was represented by a ball of tinsel hanging by a string from the rafters and illuminated with a spotlight. I have also seen the star indicated by a fascinating electronic device costing thousands of dollars; a mechanical marvel that shimmered and shone from dozens of tiny inset quartz

10. I doubt I really need to repeat this, but for heaven's sake, don't try to do this without professional help. It is extremely dangerous. See the "Miscellaneous" section of the Appendix to this book for people who specialize in human flight for the Broadway stage and Hollywood.

11. Matthew 2:1-12 tells the entire magi story.

lamps. If either of those Christmas pageants had used the star from the other, the effect would have been ludicrous, but each matched the overall style of the show. And that is, I stress again, extremely important.

The Lighting-Effect Star

Many Christmas dramas will be well-served by using one of the show's lighting instruments for the star. There are basically two ways of doing this: *into* the audience and *away from* the audience.

The "into the audience" approach may be the easiest, depending on the physical structure of the building where your drama is performed. If there is enough space above your stage, a lighting instrument can be hung above the area illuminated by your general lighting. If this instrument is aimed toward the audience and turned on at the appropriate moment, it will appear as nothing but a bright light hanging in the darkness.

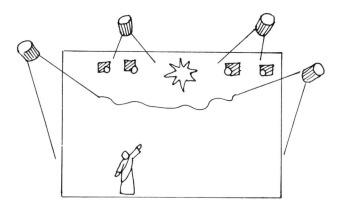

The "away from the audience" approach, depending on the design of your set and of the space where the show is being performed, uses a lighting instrument with a gobo to create a star effect. A gobo is simply a piece of fireproof metal with a pattern punched entirely through it. When this is placed at a proper distance from an intense light, the pattern is projected with sharp focus wherever the instrument happens to point.[12]

There are gobos available in the shapes of stars of all kinds, including the traditional eight-pointed Christmas star "with a tail as big as a kite." So if there is a dark, flat area anywhere above your Nativity set, a projected gobo of the star may be exactly the sign your magi have been searching for.

12. Some lighting instruments have special gobo frames or gobo slots built into them for this purpose; they hold the gobos safely and in perfect focus. See the Appendix for more information about acquiring ready-made gobos as well as books on these and other lighting effects.

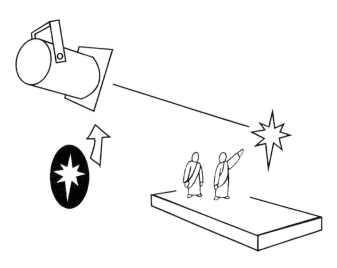

13. My favorite Bethlehem star was in a production designed after children's drawings: the set pieces were all two-dimensional cutouts painted to look like they had been drawn with crayons, and so on. At one point a little girl walked onstage carrying a white paper plate on which was painted a simple yellow, five-pointed star. She held this over her head and the three wise men followed her off. It was perfect—because it was entirely consistent with the design of the rest of the show.

14. "Tight special" describes a lighting instrument casting an extremely narrow beam on something, with no "spillover" light illuminating anything else. Many of these technical terms are defined in the Glossary at the end of this book.

15. Some pageant directors really love this effect, and many audiences seem to find it awe-inspiring. But use mirror balls with caution; many of us associate them with the disco age . . . and do not like to be reminded of *Saturday Night Fever* while contemplating the birth of Christ. See the Appendix for a source of these and other special tricks with mirrors, prisms, and so on.

The Physical-Object Star

Another approach is to construct a two-dimensional or three-dimensional star that hangs down over the stage. Here again, the design for this will be entirely dictated by the design of the rest of your production.[13]

Aluminum foil seems so mundane, and yet it is the constant source of apparent miracles in the theatre. A cardboard star covered with foil (rubber cement will hold these two surfaces together nicely) can be easily hung over the Nativity with two strings—and will still move just enough that when any light hits it, the star will shimmer and "twinkle." Just make sure that the foil has been glued on very carefully, so there are as few wrinkles as possible.

Better still—use ScotchLite (see p.15).

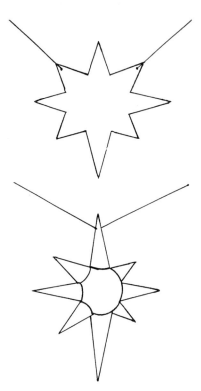

More elaborate stars are possible, of course, and can be very effective. I have seen a Bethlehem star made out of the Styrofoam cones that florists use (available at most craft and hobby stores—or from your local florist). The designer had gathered several of the longest, thinnest cones and stuck them together with pencils that had been sharpened at both ends. (I would suggest adding a few drops of an adhesive like Liquid Nails—available at all hardware stores.) The end result was shaped like the eight-pointed star pictured here and made a much more attractive-looking star than one might expect. Hanging against a black backdrop and illuminated by a tight special,[14] it was in fact quite lovely.

Some productions have employed a "mirror ball," a commercially available sphere covered with tiny mirrors. When intense light strikes any surface of the ball, tiny shards of light are reflected all over the room.[15] This can be an effective moment: the Light coming into the world and literally touching the magi—and everyone in the audience as well.

The Electric Star

For many years, people came away from productions like the Radio City Music Hall's annual Christmas spectacular with the burning desire to have an electric star in their next pageant just like the one they saw at the Music Hall. The star they had seen was a five-foot-tall construct made of molded fiberglass with dozens of intensely bright lights set into its surface. I worked on the construction of one of the many incarnations of this effect (they tended to need replacing every year) and can assure you that it is even more complex than it looks.

One challenge is to keep the framework rigid enough to hold the lights in place without becoming so heavy that it is dangerous to hang the thing over the heads of your actors. The biggest challenge, however, is to supply power to the star's light bulbs without the star obviously having a thick cable sticking out of it. There's not a very good way to put a battery pack or generator inside, since a device capable of lighting those lamps

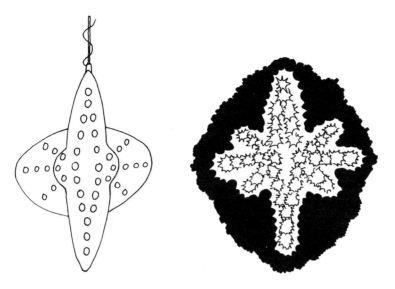

will be extremely large and/or heavy. So powering the star through a cable is necessary, but unless the set and lighting design of the rest of the stage conceals this perfectly, it can look a bit silly. Naturally using a black cable will help somewhat, but the real key is in building the rest of the design of the show around the star and keeping the other stage lights from ever shining on that cable. In any case, you should exercise great caution in keeping the star from looking like what it is: a mechanical device with light bulbs all over it.[16]

A Sky Full of Stars

An effect that often "wows" the December crowd at Radio City Music Hall is the pitch-black night sky over the Nativity, in which hundreds of twinkling stars can be seen overhead. How did we do this? And can you do it too? I'm glad you asked.

It's called a star drop, and it's basically a big sheet with light bulbs stuck through it. Of course this an understatement, but only a small one. The Music Hall star drop is about 50 feet tall and almost 100 feet wide—but it's still basically a sheet, a big piece of fabric. Big pieces of fabric are something your production can probably get, one way or another.

Flameproofed black velour is absolutely the best for a star drop. It has enough thickness to hold the lights in place (by a process I'll describe in a moment) and is heavy enough to hang straight and still, so the "sky" doesn't "ripple" every time someone walks near it. But most importantly, the *pile* of the velour absorbs light, so it is not only black but actually appears to not be there at all.

Velour can be bought on rolls of varying widths; ours came directly from the mill and was on a roll 20 feet wide. We cut this into 50-foot lengths

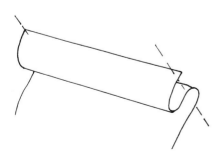

and then hemmed these panels all around, making them somewhat smaller. Then a double hem was sewn into the top to give a safe grip to the hardware that would ultimately hold the entire curtain up—making it smaller still.

We built five panels of this kind and hung them with a slight overlap like so:

16. I once heard a little boy ask his mother, as they were leaving the Music Hall's Christmas show, "Did the three wise men really see a flying saucer?" An astute question.

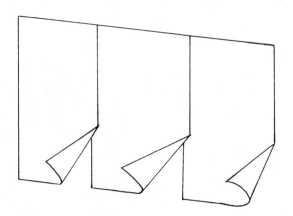

17. I mention this so you do not measure your stage's width and simply buy exactly that much cloth; you should plan to lose at least a foot on the total width of each panel. So for a stage width of 100 feet, buy enough fabric to actually cover, say, 105 feet.

18. Finding exactly the right parts was a major part of the Music Hall project, and if you plan to imitate this design you will have some serious investigative shopping to do. See the Appendix for some suggestions on where to begin the quest.

This subtracted still more overall width.[17] The panels were fitted with matching strips of Velcro fasteners so they could be quickly and easily attached in series. This prevented the possibility of an accidental "tear" appearing in the sky!

If you plan to build a drop like this, there are special lamps and their sockets to consider.[18] The size of the lamp will be determined by the relative size of the "stars" you need for the space in which the drop will be hung. I recommend setting up several sizes of lamps on your darkened stage and then viewing them from the back-most seat in the house. Which of these lamps looks the most like a star in the night sky?

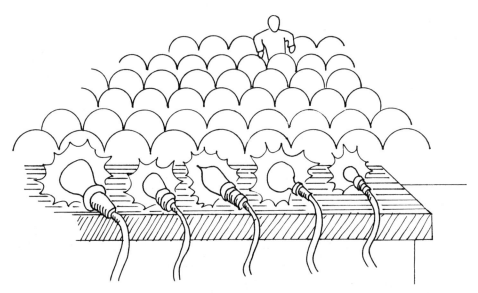

Once you have selected your lamp, you are ready to find a base, or socket, that will not only hold the lamp and allow easy wiring but also allow easy attachment to the grommets you're going to hammer into the drop. (More about that in a moment.)

The sockets we used on our drop had a screw-on ring like this

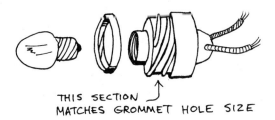

THIS SECTION MATCHES GROMMET HOLE SIZE

that allowed us to secure them firmly to the drop by simply pushing the threaded end through the grommet and screwing the ring back on.

We had already drawn a plan showing the exact placement of all the stars we wanted to show. Using this as our guide, we laid the velour panels out and stuck round labels on the places where we wanted to "plant" a light bulb.[19] Once we had these spots marked, we were able to start punching the holes. This involved a piece of heavy-duty machinery: a hole punch with a large enough "mouth" to allow yards of velour to be bundled up inside it.

19. The Avery company makes adhesive colored dots that work perfectly for this purpose—their glue sticks to the velour when you want it to, but peels off leaving very little residue.

These will be available at any good office-supply store. Our biggest challenge at this point of the construction was finding a room large enough to allow us to spread this gi-ant dropout on the floor!

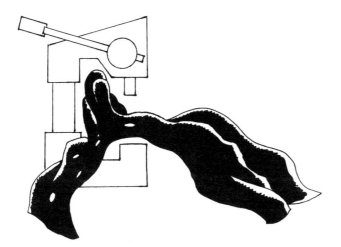

While one worker was punching holes, another followed along behind and hammered grommets into them. We had selected grommets based on the size and shape of the lamps and sockets we planned to use. This step is important; the fit of all of these parts must be as exact as possible to insure the lamps will stay in place.

Then each socket was connected to the drop and wired into the power strip that would connect to the Music Hall's lighting control system. (If you're not an expert in electrical wiring, you must have the help of someone who is.) We added an additional effect by wiring each socket on one of three different circuits, chosen at random.

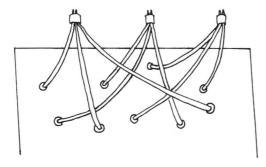

If you wire your drop this way, the level of power going to each group of lights can be controlled independently of the others, allowing for a wide variety of "star fields" on the same drop.

Now at last you can screw in all the lamps. They can be of any color you choose—white or clear will be fine, but randomly adding some yellows, reds, and blues will be more realistic and appealing.

I should mention that a star drop of this kind requires special care in storage. First you should remove all the lamps. Then the curtain should be gently folded like so:

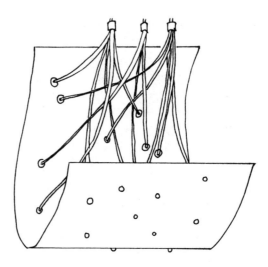

and stored either in a crate or in some place where nothing else will ever rest on top of it. Otherwise the connections between the wires and the sockets will probably be damaged.

A Couple of Miracles

A passion play cannot do justice to the life of Christ without representing the miracles of Jesus. Unfortunately, this calls for you, the special effects artist and prop master, to either produce some genuine miracles for each performance of the show or somehow simulate them.

Let's assume, for the sake of discussion, that you plan to simulate them.

There are many to choose from! Some—like walking on the water—are rarely written into passion-play scripts. When they *are* included, they are usually accompanied by some suggestions as to how the effect should be presented. Others are almost universally used in most passion plays. So let's concentrate on the two most often included in passion-play and Easter drama scripts: the miracle at the wedding at Cana and the feeding of the 5,000.

Water into Wine

The scenario is this: there are six large vessels that Jesus has told the steward to fill with water. When a sample is drawn out of the pitcher, it is no longer water but wine.[20]

20. Described only in John 2:1-11. The solution to this effects problem seemed obvious to me—once I went back to Scripture and read the story closely. A valuable lesson, that.

Here is a case where the director and other designers must be consulted. What exactly will these vessels look like? Will we *see* the wine being tasted? Will we *see* the water being poured into the jug—and the wine being drawn out? If not, your actors can simply look in the pot and say, "It's water" and then look into the ladle or pitcher and say, "It's a miracle! It's wine!"

If you want the audience to *see* the water turned into wine, the easiest method seems to be some sort of powder (such as instant fruit drink mix) placed in the pots so that when the clear water is poured in, the mixture will turn red. And if none of the actors are expected to drink this, tempera paint or other thick, soluble dyes could be used. I have attempted this "mix as you go" method but have never found a balance of water-to-coloring that will blend thoroughly just by pouring the water over the coloring. You may have better luck in your experiments! I hope so—because when it works well, adding a coloring to the water is a perfect solution (chemistry pun intended).

I have seen a more dramatic method work quite impressively. It requires a good deal more preparation—and the construction of a special prop. But you may find it worth all the effort.

The trick is based on a large pot that has a built-in divider, making it two vessels in one.

One compartment is filled with clear water, the other with wine (or whatever is chosen to look like wine). The effect works like this: Jesus has the steward show what is in the pot, and the steward dips into the pot with a narrow pitcher and draws out water—which he pours into cups that Jesus and the disciples hold. Then Jesus has the steward repeat the process. This time the steward dips into the "wine side" of the pot—and pours the deep red liquid into the cups, giving the audience plenty of time to see the different-colored stream as the wine is poured.[21]

This is that rare effect that will work beautifully on a small-stage, low-budget production as well as in a megabucks outdoor-drama passion play extravaganza.

The Loaves and Fishes

No matter what size Christ-narrative drama you are staging, you probably will not have 5,000 people onstage at any time. (Even the colossal passion play at Oberammergau doesn't have 5,000 actors!) But assuming you can have, say, *30* people onstage, an enactment of the feeding of the 5,000[22] can be very powerful—if the effect of the multiplying food is well-handled.

The best trick I've ever heard of for multiplying the loaves and fishes involves the use of some cunningly cut and painted pieces of *sponge rubber* (that springy, extremely porous material commonly used in upholstery and available at most large fabric stores).

The foam is simply cut into these shapes and painted with a *latex* paint[23] to resemble bread and fish. Once dry, these pieces of sponge rub-

21. I once made this effect work with a trick pitcher that had two holding tanks and button-controlled electrical pumps to force first water, then wine, to the mouth of the pitcher. This is what is known as "overkill." (It also only worked about three-fourths of the time.) There are certainly other options that work just as well and are less expensive—and are not so hard on the props and effects team.

22. As in Matthew 14:13-21, Mark 6:32-44, Luke 9:10-17, and John 6:1-15. The details differ somewhat, but the essence of the story is identical in all Gospel sources.

23. Enamel paints will either refuse to dry on the sponge rubber or will degrade the rubber into an ugly mess of slime. Experiment with various latex paints— you'll find a good match eventually.

ber can be easily compacted into extremely small "pellets" or "wads" and kept in the palm of the hand.

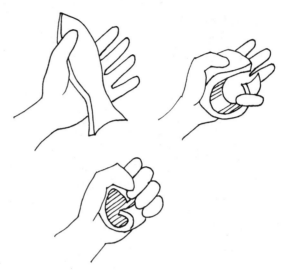

24. This idea was suggested to me by someone at Lillenas's 1995 Drama in the Church Workshop. Since I cannot recall who it was, I apologize to that creative individual for my not being able to give credit where it is due. In any event, I thank you for sharing this ingenious idea—and I expect countless others who try this will thank you as well. See Part Three of this book for some help with sleight of hand tricks such as "producing" these loaves and fishes "from thin air." See the Appendix for books on blocking these kinds of crowd scenes.

25. And when the scene was over, one of the disciples picked the basket up and carried it offstage in such a way that we in the audience could clearly see the large hole in its bottom. This illustrates the importance of carefully explaining every special effect of this kind to every cast or crew member who will have anything to do with it. Sometimes you may have to explain it several times.

26. The three effects discussed in this section might seem to belong in the next part of this book, since they all involve specially constructed props. But they also require the practiced participation of the actors in the scene—and that makes them special effects.

27. In John 18:10, anyway. In the other Gospel accounts neither the disciple who attacks nor the victim are named. It is generally assumed that John is simply giving the most complete version of this incident.

28. At least he does in Luke 22:49-51.

So the disciples reach into their basket and hand out what appears to be five loaves and two fish. Each of these is passed from one actor to another, while the compressed foam pieces they have held are allowed to expand in the actors' hands. With a little careful blocking and some practiced sleight of hand, each member of your crowd may seem to approach the disciples with empty hands and then be seen a moment later holding an armload of food.[24]

I have also seen this miracle attempted with various trick baskets. One show I witnessed had their Philip carry an unlikely looking wicker affair easily big enough to carry dozens of good-sized fish sandwiches, but in which he had claimed to have only five pieces of bread and a pair of fish. So when the disciples pulled out a multitude of bread and fish, we in the audience were not especially surprised.

A slightly more convincing option has been used on stages that are equipped with *traps*—panels of the stage floor that can be temporarily removed. In one production I saw, the "five loaves and two fish" basket was left on the floor throughout the feeding of the multitude while the disciples reached into it again and again. The basket had a hole in the bottom that set over an open trap in the stage. A stagehand was under that floor, handing up loaf after loaf, fish after fish.[25]

The Arrest and Persecution of Jesus[26]

Now we must move from the lighthearted to the most serious of all: Gethsemane, Jerusalem, and finally Golgotha. Depending on the script, your Easter drama may not have demanded much of the special-effects department up until now. If so, that is all about to change.

Cutting Off Malchus's Ear

When Jesus is arrested, Peter lashes out with his sword and cuts off the ear of a man named Malchus, a slave of the high priest.[27] Scripture then tells us that Jesus *heals* Malchus.[28] If your script calls for this, you may be happy to know that there is at least one tried-and-true method for handling such a thing.

When Peter enters this scene, he has two props: his sword—and

Malchus's ear. Not the actor's real one, of course, but an exact duplicate made of foam latex painted the same color as the actor playing Malchus.[29] Peter keeps this palmed until he attacks Malchus. Then he makes a swipe with the sword—toward the actor but safely downstage of him, during which: (1) Malchus screams and presses his hand to the side of his head as if to stop the bleeding, and (2) Peter drops the false ear onto the ground near Malchus.

Jesus chastises Peter and picks up the fallen ear. He brings it up to the side of Malchus's head—covering it with his own palm at the last instant—then both Jesus and Malchus remove their hands from Malchus's head and *voilà!* Malchus's ear has seemingly been restored.

As he removes his hand from Malchus's head, the actor playing Jesus "palms" the ear and holds it until the next time he is offstage—which should be very soon. If not, any of the soldiers handling him can take the ear from him while holding his wrists in place for manacles, or some similar piece of business. In any case, someone then takes the ear offstage and immediately back to the prop master before it is lost.[30]

Jesus Is Flogged

Tradition plays a heavy role in our understanding of the shameful physical abuse Jesus endures at this point in the story. The Hollywood films based loosely on the life of Christ may well have colored our mental image more than anything. And the four Gospels do not entirely agree on all details here: Jesus seems to have been abused by Herod and his soldiers;[31] to have been whipped by Pilate's men prior to being condemned to crucifixion;[32] or He may have been beaten *after* sentence was passed.[33] It is possible that He endured such treatment on all three occasions.

In any case, it is the scourging after sentencing that is most often depicted onstage and is the most difficult to present effectively without obvious fakery or injury to any of the performers. Since the Bible does not describe the whipping in detail, we are left to rely on history, tradition, and surmise—all of which seem to point to the *flagrum*.

The flagrum was a nasty device that must have been dreamed up by a particularly sadistic Roman soldier; leather cords were tied together into a whip, each lash capped off with a tiny dumbbell-shaped piece of metal or bone that would strike the skin like a bullet over and over again.

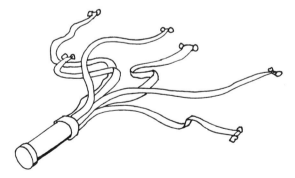

Roman soldiers believed (perhaps from experience) that receiving 40 lashes with a flagrum would kill a man. So they devised the ultimate cruelty: the "forty lashes save one." Thirty-nine lashes left the victim longing for death. This is why passion plays often depict the scourging of Jesus with 39 lashes striking His back.[34]

29. See the Appendix for sources on foam latex and the paints you'll need to match the color of this artificial part with the actor's makeup.

See Part Two of this book for a discussion of making false body parts, such as a detached Head of John the Baptist.

30. I have also seen this exact blocking used when the fallen part of the ear was simply mimed—the actor playing Jesus pretended to pick something up and pretended to reattach it to Malchus's head. And I have to admit this was very nearly as effective as using the prop.

31. Suggested in Luke 23:11.

32. Matthew 27:24-26 and Mark 15:15 described Jesus as being "scourged."

33. Matthew 27:27-31, Mark 15:16-20, and John 19:2-3 are in agreement that Jesus was beaten by the soldiers, either with their fists or with a stick.

34. And in performance, I have seen this business take as long as five minutes—seeming to go on forever. This illustrates the point that special effects exist in all dimensions, including time. If your effect is onstage for more than a minute or two, weigh it against the rest of the presentation and consider whether or not it has "stolen the show."

One gripping sequence in the rock opera *Jesus Christ Superstar* makes dramatic use of the "39 lashes," but in that script there is music under all the action and an important emotional moment for Pontius Pilate, all during the scourging. Even with all of that, 39 of anything takes time.

Assuming this is something you want to show in your passion play, how can it be done without hurting anyone?

The bottom line is this: it's not "safe" to hit *anybody* with *anything,* on the stage or anywhere else. There is always something that can go wrong, such as the "victim" accidentally being hit in the eye. No matter what an actor is hit with, real injury is possible. But if your actor portraying Jesus is amenable to a certain amount of risk and suffering (and if he isn't he probably wouldn't have taken on this most difficult of all roles in the first place), forge ahead—carefully.

First of all, what exactly does this effect need to *look* and *sound* like?

If Jesus was beaten with a flagrum, He would have been left with bloody stripes on His back[35] and scores of tiny red welts at the end of each stripe. Each lash would have made a sound like splintering wood, a sharp "crack!" ending with the cry of the victim.

The challenge of achieving these results without injury to the actor was given to me when I was effects designer for a passion play performed in an outdoor arena. The effect needed to be realistic, it needed to be foolproof, and it needed to be easily seen by audience members on the back row—about 200 feet from the stage. The actors playing Jesus and the soldier, along with the director, costume designer, props master, makeup artist, and myself all met together to discuss how this could be done. We brainstormed and experimented day after day. Through this process of trial and error we at last arrived at a solution that was rather involved but produced a powerful effect.[36]

We cut strips of brown felt approximately one yard long and one inch wide. Then we fastened small cotton-yarn pom-poms (cut from a pair of little girls' socks) to one end of each. The other end we bundled into a thin plastic bottle, similar to a restaurant ketchup dispenser. This bottle was filled with stage blood, and the lashes of the whip were dipped in stage blood as well, just before the "scourging" was about to begin.[37] When the whip was slapped across the actor's back, red stripes with small red globules on one end were left behind.

35. Many versions of Isaiah 53:5 read "by his stripes we are healed." If your presentation of this scene does nothing but illuminate that text for your audience, you will have something to rejoice over.

36. In case you have not read the introduction to this book, I would encourage you to do so at this point. Some very important ramifications of this particular effect are discussed.

37. Actually, in our earliest experiments, the handle was made of wood, and we simply dipped the felt and pompom into stage blood. Later we discovered that the felt tended to dry out quickly, so we substituted the wooden handle with the plastic bottle and filled it with diluted stage blood so the whip could be "inked" whenever someone squeezed the bottle.

The lashes were long enough to look dangerous but wide enough that they were unlikely to actually inflict pain on the actor being whipped. The "little red dots" on the end of the felt strips were surprisingly visible, even from the back rows of the amphitheatre.

We had to experiment extensively to find the right balance of fluid. If the lash had too little stage blood on it, it would not produce the desired effect. Too much, and it hurled thick red drops into the audience with each swing. But eventually we found the exact quantity needed, and simply measured out that amount for each performance.

There was, however, one major problem remaining: it didn't make a noise. The "smack" of the whip connecting with the man's back would have to come from somewhere besides the actual impact—but where?

We considered all the pieces we had at hand. We had the whip; having it somehow make the noise was ruled out. We had the soldier. There also seemed to be no way to have him make the noise. Then we realized we also had the man being beaten and that his hands were not visible to the audience.

So we outfitted the whipping-post with a slap-stick. It was in fact a paint-stirring stick given to us at the local hardware store, attached to the post with the spring-clasp mechanism we cut off of a clipboard. The actor playing Jesus pulled the stick away from the post, putting tension on the spring, and the soldier gave him verbal cues—"Now!" he would say (in a voice the audience could not hear) as he was bringing the whip down. The actor then released the stick

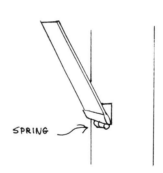

just when the soldier brought the whip down—CRACK! It took a lot of practice for the two of them to get perfectly synchronized, but by opening night it was so convincing that some of us began to worry that the dye in the felt lashes of the whip had started to stiffen, turning the prop whip into a *real* one.

The Crown of Thorns

The final act of ridicule from Pilate's soldiers is to place a mock crown on Jesus' head—a crown made of plaited thorns, which we must assume brought blood at every part of His head that it touched.[38] For many people, the image of Jesus wearing a crown of thorns that causes drops of blood to run down His face like tears is a powerful and important one.

Our crown of thorns worked on very much the same principle as the

38. Matthew 27:29, Mark 15:17, and John 19:2 are virtually identical in their description of the crown, but they give no details. So once again we must use our imaginations.

whip in the previous section. As with the whip, this prop was designed to leave traces of stage blood, and to be under the control of the actor playing one of the soldiers.

The crown was made of hollow plastic tubing about one-eighth of an inch in diameter. A length of perhaps five feet had been twisted into an overlapping coil the size of the head of the actor playing Jesus. One end was melted closed; the other was left open, poking up through the tangle of tubing.

The spikes of the thorns themselves were made of tiny slivers of PlasterCraft plaster bandage (see p. 48), which stuck to the tubing just fine once it, too, was entirely covered with a thin coating of PlasterCraft. The whole construction was then painted dark brown.

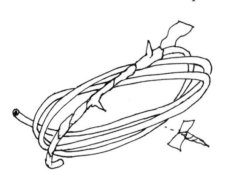

Now tiny holes were carefully poked into the underside of the tubing with an extremely sharp X-acto knife. Since it would be sheer surface tension that would keep the stage blood inside the tubing, it was safest to start with the tiniest holes possible and experiment with enlarging them later.

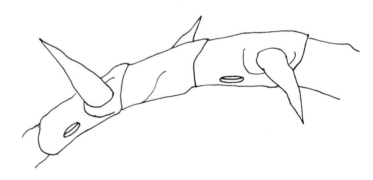

39. Squeeze bulbs have all kinds of uses in special effects. I use the kind that are made for spraying nose drops into baby's noses. In fact, the "baby needs" section of a well-stocked drugstore is a veritable treasure trove for the props and effects designer. Strange but true.

40. As you might imagine, this took a good deal of practice to make perfect. At first the holes were so small no stage blood could get through; later we made the holes so big the blood simply ran out as soon as it was pumped in. Then we made a new crown with the right size holes and a much larger pump. When we squeezed this high-volume bulb the crown sent stage blood spraying in all directions. Hardly consistent with the intended gravity of the moment onstage.

Just before the crown was to be brought onstage, we filled the tubing with stage blood using a hand-operated squeeze pump, a small bulb[39] that fitted on the open end of the tubing. One stagehand squeezed the fluid into the crown while another held the ends of her fingers over the holes. Once the tubing was completely full, the bulb was detached, completely filled again, and reattached. The soldier then brought this overloaded structure onstage and pressed it down onto Jesus' head. As he pushed down, he gave the bulb a squeeze, forcing some of the stage blood from the tubing through the holes . . . and slowly trickling down the brow of Jesus. When he released the crown he took the bulb off, palming it until he got offstage.[40]

The Crucifixion and Death of Jesus

The exact sequence of events on the day of Jesus' crucifixion has been discussed, researched, and speculated upon as much as any other single aspect of the life of Christ. One result of this is that your local library should be loaded with books, pamphlets, and articles on the history and traditions of crucifixions—probably everything you could want to know about what this terrible event was actually like, down to the finest detail. And if you have been given the job of creating an effective, realistic, and accurate "crucifixion" for your Easter drama, you will no doubt want to know all you can about what you're trying to re-create.[41]

An entire book could be written on the staging of this single sequence in the Easter drama.[42] For the sake of brevity, let's concentrate only on the part that usually causes the most concern for directors, designers, and actors alike: the nailing of the hands and feet of Jesus.

At the Cross

There is a quick, easy solution to the problem of simulating the piercing of Jesus' hands and feet, and it has been well and widely used in generations of passion plays. The soldier who will drive the nails is blocked in such a way that he eclipses his own work.

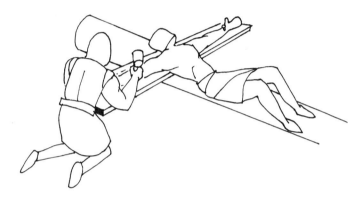

From this position the soldier can drive the nails into the cross-beam, hammering them down very close to the hands and feet of Jesus. This way the general body positioning is convincing, and the sounds are thoroughly authentic.

Keeping the actual impact point of the nails obscured has its positive and negative aspects. On the one hand, it's usually considered bad blocking to put an actor's back between the audience and a very important piece of stage business. On the other hand, if your director feels that the production should not dwell too much on the blood-and-gore aspects of the Crucifixion, this allows the audience to know exactly what is happening without being forced to see a man suffer while having a spike driven through his wrist.

There are passion plays in which the driving of the nails is not seen at all. They handle the sequence this way: after the scene in which Jesus is sentenced to death, all the stage lights fade to black. Then in the darkness we *hear* the nails being driven—and the cries of the man whose flesh is pierced in the process.[43] After a moment, the lights onstage fade up to reveal the traditional Crucifixion tableau: Jesus on the Cross, the two thieves on either side. A very effective way of clearing the stage for a complicated scene change, this approach offers all the advantages and none of the disadvantages of deliberately blocking the audience's view. Instead of *looking* like a "special effect in progress," the blackout simply encourages the audience to use their imaginations.[44]

The Spikes. Neither of these solutions, though, allow for showing the heads of the spikes in Jesus' hands and feet. One method for doing this would be to fabricate three false spike heads, either carved of light wood such as balsa, or even cast in rubber such as latex. These pieces would then be glued with liquid latex to the parts of the actor's body where the

41. Although it's not actually a book about the Crucifixion, my favorite discussion of the topic is in Ian Wilson's fascinating book *The Mysterious Shroud* (Doubleday, 1986). Perhaps the most complete examination in print of the legendary Shroud of Turin, it studies in detail the artifact that may yet prove to be a "photograph" of the scourged and bloodied body of Jesus.

42. I suggest looking at the various ways this has been handled in motion pictures, some of which were very carefully researched and skillfully carried out. I recommend *Jesus of Nazareth*, the Genesis Project's fine film *Jesus, The Greatest Story Ever Told*, and especially the Nicholas Ray film *King of Kings*. The most historically accurate Crucifixion is probably the one depicted in the controversial film *The Last Temptation of Christ* and may be quite surprising if your mental image has been influenced by medieval religious paintings. They were rarely based on any research at all.

43. The sounds recorded on the Lillenas CD *Sound Effects for Seasonal Productions* are extremely useful for making this effect work.

44. While a lengthy blackout always makes an audience uncomfortable, this one must be of sufficient length for the entire scene change to be completed. I once saw a passion play that used this effect, and one night the lights came up to reveal one of the thieves not yet up on his cross, one foot still on the ground. To make matters worse, the soldier guarding him tried to save the scene by prodding the thief with his spear and snarling, "Get up there!" Which the thief obligingly did. It was very hard to take anything else in the scene seriously after that.

spike has supposedly penetrated. If he keeps his hands and feet still—and perfectly flush against the cross—this effect can be quite striking. But it does require a good deal of time; the latex has to dry and this operation can hardly be performed onstage. So this would only work in a production that has several scenes prior to the Crucifixion in which Jesus was offstage.

One particularly ingenious solution involves a specially made spike that fits over the hand of the actor playing Jesus. It is a piece of specially forged iron that will not bend closed on the actor's hand, even while being driven into a heavy piece of wood. Once the spike has been well-seated into the crossbeam, the actor conceals the bent portion of the spike with his own thumb.

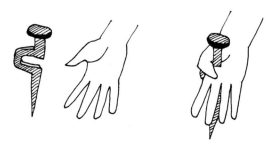

In some versions of this device, a variation on the same piece is used on his crossed ankles with a rough piece of wood covering part of the spike. This is even harder to drive into the cross than the spike with the U-shape cast into it, but with practice these can be very effective.[45]

45. Here the services of a professional blacksmith will be invaluable, since it seems best to have these specially made to fit the hand of the actor playing Jesus, and of the exact size and thickness you desire.

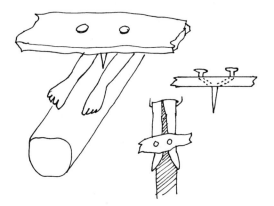

Hanging on the Cross. Important as all of these "tricks with the nails" may be, none of them addresses the problem of getting a normal-sized human actor to convincingly hang on a cross without actually doing injury to him.

Some medieval paintings show the crucified men "standing" on a small platform nailed to the face of the cross. Others also show the men's arm's tied to the crossbeam with ropes. Since the main idea of crucifixion was to cause the condemned to die very, very slowly, these additions are not at all unlikely—and can help greatly in keeping your actor safely where he needs to be when performing this scene.

I recommend using the ropes, if for no other reason than they will help keep your actor safe. They will also cover a multitude of sins at the places where you have pretended to drive nails through his body.

Of course this whole problem is aggravated by the need for the actor to be nearly nude, leaving fewer places to hide things.[46] In fact Roman history suggests that those condemned to crucifixion were in fact further shamed by being nailed up fully naked, but fortunately for the effects designer a tradition has arisen that Jesus wore a simple sort of loincloth while on the Cross. I have seen this used to help solve the problem of keeping the actor on the cross, with the loincloth covering a sort of harness custom-built for the actor's comfort and safety. The whole affair was then attached to a clasp on the face of the cross during the "driving the spikes" scene.

46. Probably the ultimate demonstration of this is in the 1981 John Boorman film *Excalibur*. We see Sir Lancelot—totally nude—pierced by the famous sword, the blade emerging through a gash in his back, then drawn back out again. There's no place to hide any "trick blade," and this was long before the kind of computer-enhanced visual effects we see today. I used to arrogantly claim that I could explain any special effect on stage or screen—but I shut up after seeing this part of *Excalibur*. If you know how this effect was achieved, please let me know. It's driving me crazy.

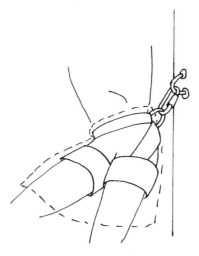

Even if you haven't tried this, you can imagine that this device has to be constructed and used very carefully. Since much of that actor's weight will be suspended inside this "yoke," it is crucial that he be comfortable, able to maintain good blood circulation, be held securely to the cross, and not liable to turn upside down should he lose his footing.[47] As usual, trial and error will yield the best results.

The most ingenious solution I've ever encountered to all of these problems is a specially constructed cross fitted with prosthetic duplicates of the hands of the actor playing Jesus. These were permanently mounted to the cross, the wrists obscured by a bundle of thick ropes. During a blackout that began the scene, the actor would reach into a cavity inside the cross-beam and pull himself into position by grabbing handles that

47. Perhaps the best arrangement of this harness can be suggested by someone interested in the sport of rappelling. This is very similar to the rig they use, and it is perfectly capable of supporting the actor's weight and of holding him right-side-up.

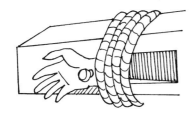 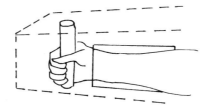

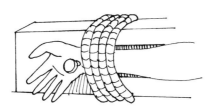

48. If you want to attempt this, be sure to see the last section of the Props part of this book for a discussion of making foamed-rubber duplicates of body parts.

have been built into the hollow structure. The lights would then rise and the soldiers could be seen driving the spikes into (what appeared to be) Jesus' hands! The cross was then raised, the actor apparently attached to the cross solely by the ropes and by the nails through his palms.[48]

A Different View. Mention should be made here of a completely different approach: setting the cross up so Jesus' back is to the audience. This frees you for all manner of simpler methods of keeping the actor on the cross and from having to worry about whether or not the spikes actually appear to penetrate his hands or feet. In addition, it throws the focus away from Jesus (whose last words can still be heard) and on to those who have come to see Him—the mockers, John the disciple, the centurion, and of course Mary, mother of Jesus. Many passion plays present the Crucifixion this way, and it can be immensely powerful.

The Spear

49. Described only in John 19:31-37.

A quick description should be made here of one method for dealing with the spear that pierces Jesus' side.[49] This is a variation of the old "stage blood knife" that has been used since the days of Shakespeare—basically a fancy squirt gun.

The shaft is one-inch-diameter pipe of light metal or the common PVC used in household plumbing. A piece of soft, flexible plastic has been cut into a spearhead shape and attached to one end of the shaft like this:

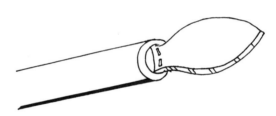

Also at that end a bulb full of stage blood has been securely attached to the inside, and a dowel with wood disks at either end has been fitted behind the bulb.

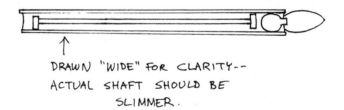

DRAWN "WIDE" FOR CLARITY--
ACTUAL SHAFT SHOULD BE
SLIMMER.

The soldier carrying the spear presses the head against Jesus' side and simultaneously pushes in on the end of the dowel. This squeezes the blood out of the bulb and down Jesus' side. It also obscures the point of the spear, so it is less obvious that the point has not punctured the actor's skin.

Signs in the Sky

50. Matthew 27:45, Mark 15:33, and Luke 23:44.
51. Matthew 27:51.

Three of the Gospels[50] tell us that the Crucifixion was marked in the heavens by a sudden darkness, like a solar eclipse. Matthew goes on to record an earthquake following Jesus' death.[51] The degree to which you may attempt these things depends on the style and limitations of your overall production. Earthquakes have always been particularly difficult to represent onstage, and unless you can somehow shake the audience as well as the stage, I have little to suggest except for indicating the quake with a loud noise instead of physical movement.[52]

52. Here again, the *Sound Effects for Seasonal Productions* CD from Lillenas is most helpful.

The sudden darkness is more complicated than simply dimming all the stage lights. (You probably don't want to black out the stage while so much important action is going on.) If your lighting plot will allow it, I suggest an arrangement similar to this:

So that when the sky darkens, the effect onstage is a slow fade to dark except for the small specials on some of the principal characters.

This can be a very evocative image: the rest of the world falls into darkness—only the sacrifice of Jesus remains visible. And in one of the few other pools of light we see also the centurion, who proclaims Jesus to be the Son of God.[53] Fade to black.

53. As in Mark 15:39.

Resurrection and Ascension

Congratulations—you survived the darkest part of this process. Onward to the Resurrection!

The Stone Rolls Away

Some passion play scripts call for the stone to be seen rolling away from tomb, either under the influence of an angel[54] or apparently by itself. Whether or not you plan to do this, now is a good time for you and your

54. For those who prefer Matthew's telling of the story.

scenic designer to consider just what the tomb and the stone should look like. One suggestion: the tomb set and the stone effect are classic examples of stage pieces that can be made using blown fiberglass.[55] But what shape to have fiberglass blown into?

55. See Part Three of this book for an extensive discussion of blown fiberglass.

History and tradition generally agree that the stones used to seal tombs in first-century Judea were carved for the purpose, not simply boulders rolled over the mouth of a cave. They would have been almost-perfectly round disks, flat on both sides—like enormous coins.

Depending on the size you want and the weight you are willing to contend with, the framework can be constructed of "chicken wire" (the wire used in making fences around chicken coops) or of wood.

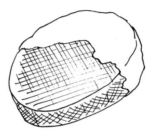 

The fiberglass should be blown over this randomly, making sure to build up an irregular surface pitted with grooves and mottled with lumps so it will not look as if it was cut with 20th-century tools.

A lower-budget (but more time-consuming) alternative is to cover the framework with papier-mâché or PlasterCraft.[56] Neither of these surfaces will be as rigid as the fiberglass.

56. See the Appendix for sources of these materials.

Now the entire "stone" should be painted (along with the exterior of the tomb). This paint should be *sprayed* on—not brushed—to get the mottled colors seen in natural stone. The colors, of course, will depend on the design of your set or the kind of stone you want to emulate.

If the stone is light enough, it can be moved with a simple strand of fishing line pulled by someone offstage.

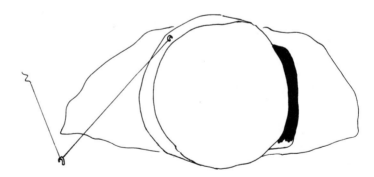

For heavier "stones" a more complex method is required. One solution might be called "the clever lever"—a concealed seesaw that is built into the set and can be operated from offstage and on cue.

Both of these methods can be used with an angel onstage, giving him or her the appearance of superhuman strength. Of course, depending on the weight and design of the stone, your angel may well be able to roll it away from the tomb without help.

Take care that your stone is at least heavy enough to keep it from bouncing when it falls over. Be sure that the set design includes a logical

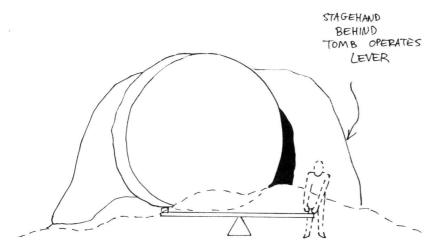

STAGEHAND
BEHIND
TOMB OPERATES
LEVER

place for the stone to *stop*—you don't want it to get away and roll into the audience.

Angels and Light

Speaking of the angel(s)[57] at the tomb, here again are messengers with apparel that shines like lightning. As with the angels that visit Mary and Joseph, I recommend coordinating with your costume and lighting designers to make this effect work.[58]

Many Easter dramas feature an open tomb with some kind of light streaming out from within. Whether your lighting source is a 1,000-watt lamp, a campfire, or a helium-neon laser, it will be the "streaming out" part of the effect that will pose a problem. Light normally tends to spread out rather than *focus,* so it needs to be helped along if it's going to appear to be powerful rays of energy. One of the easiest ways to make light beams show up where you want them is to give them something to shine onto—such as stage fog.

Stage fog gets it name from the atmospheric condition it's most often used to imitate, but it's not really fog. It's a chemically produced vapor that is perfectly harmless to everyone except the most sensitive. Special machines[59] spray the compound into the air quickly and silently, and in a building with a large air-conditioning system the vapor can be easily dispersed.

Once the air is "fogged" (and experimentation will tell you what level of density is best for your purposes) all light entering the foggy area will focus into coherent streams of light. So if the air around your Easter Sunday tomb has been fogged, when the stone rolls away and lights inside shine out, well-defined rays will shine out like searchlights (provided the lights are substantially brighter than the lights everywhere else onstage).

57. Once again, depending on which Gospel your drama is based upon. In Matthew 28 and Mark 16, there is one angel; in Luke 24 there are two. In John 20, there is no angel at all!

58. See the first section of Part One of this book, "What Should Your Angels Look Like?"

59. See the Appendix for sources.

Taken Up into Heaven

The final special effect called for in the Christ story is that of the Ascension. In the full sight of His disciples, Jesus is taken up into heaven. So how to present this onstage?

In some passion plays the Ascension is treated as simply another exit: Jesus exits stage left, then two angels enter, asking the disciples why they're standing around looking up into the sky? Sometimes we in the audience wonder the same thing. It's certainly an anticlimactic way to end the greatest story ever told.[60]

As we discussed earlier, flying rigs can be used to make human performers seem to rise into the air. They are expensive, and they are dangerous—but it is certainly an impressive effect. The Ascension may pose a special "flying" challenge, however Jesus must rise into the air and then *disappear.*

A better alternative may be another that I mentioned earlier: using a scenic scrim for dramatic revelations.[61]

Onstage, a "revelation" is the sudden and dramatic appearance of a person or object. The drama also works in reverse: the audience can be astounded by the instant *dis*appearance of a person or object, and a scrim can help make this possible. The scenario would work like this: the disciples would congregate downstage of the scrim, waiting for Jesus to appear. The lights would be up on them but dark upstage of the scrim.

Then the lights on the disciples would begin to dim as tight specials upstage of the scrim began to fade up. Jesus would be on a raised platform, the lights upstage of the scrim illuminating him and nothing else. To the audience this would appear as Jesus floating in the air over the heads—and upstage—of the disciples.

Then Jesus would speak his parting lines . . . and the lights on the

disciples would fade up to full as the lights on Jesus faded down. The effect of this would be of a bright light in the sky taking the place of Jesus—who is hidden from sight as if a cloud had come between him and the disciples.

And that's it—you've handled all the special effects for your seasonal gospel drama. Now you can concentrate on the relatively easy part: *props*.

Part Two

Props

As used in the theatre, "prop" is short for "property"—it's something that belongs to someone. In the world of biblical drama, props are usually things belonging to someone who lives in first-century Judea, a world very much different from our own.

Happily, many of the things that people really owned in that place and time have survived, so we can look at them and see what they were like, how they were made, and how they were used.[1] From this we can surmise a lot about what the things that did *not* survive were like.

1. The Appendix lists references for the study of life in "Bible Times."

The challenge of the property master or props designer for a biblical drama is to create pieces that are authentic, durable, and within the limits of budget and schedule. Very often you may have to settle for two out of three. But with a little ingenuity you may also be able to get 100% every time.

Let's go through the Christ story chronologically again, this time focusing on the special props that your seasonal drama or passion play will probably call for.

Shepherds' Crooks

The Gospel of Luke does not tell us specifically that the shepherds had these, but it's a pretty sure bet they did. The "crooks" were the trademark of the sheep-herding profession, the handy all-purpose tool. Their distinguishing feature was the curve at one end, the "extension hand" so often needed in this line of work:

And as you might guess, walking through the woods until you find a stick shaped like that can be a fool's errand. So you'll probably have to make them. Try a piece of flexible metal pipe, such as copper or brass (available at almost any hardware store). Bend the "crook" into one end, then wrap the entire length of the pipe with ParisCraft or papier-mâché. Be sure to add plenty of lumps and knobs so it looks like something that once grew, not a piece of pipe with gunk on it. When the covering is dry, paint it realistic colors.

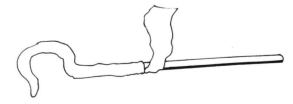

One advantage of this method is that the crooks can be custom-built to the suit the actor who will carry it. If this is an adult drama, you can make large ones; if it is a children's Nativity, you can have kid-size shepherds' crooks.

The Manger

Personal taste often becomes a major factor in designing or directing a show of this kind. One good example of this is the question of whether or not you should imitate centuries of classical religious art and endow your Holy Family with halos. Generally this arises regarding the presence of the Christ child in the manger. Is He even visible? Or is He indicated by a soft, warm light radiating from the swaddling clothes down in the hay?

Assuming that this is what you want to do, you may as well build this effect right into the manger. A manger is just a feeding-box for cattle, so it can look like almost anything—but the tradition is that it should look like this:

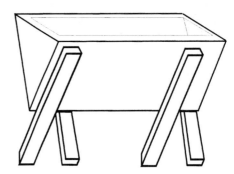

If you build yours according to this design, you can make it with as few as eight pieces of any wood you happen to have on hand—in fact the older the better.

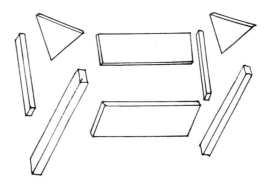

2. See the Glossary for a definition and the Appendix for sources.

Leave room for an electrical cord, because in this manger you can place a small but powerful lighting instrument such as a 6" Fresnel.[2] As long as the instrument itself is not visible to the audience, the light can be faded up and down with the beginning and ending of the scene. Or Mary can gently place the (baby doll) infant Jesus in the manger—and the lighting operator can sneak the light up as everyone gazes down into it adoringly. The success or failure of this effect will depend in some part on the blocking of the scene, since the light will mostly be seen as reflected in the faces of people nearest the manger.

An important warning, though: lighting instruments get *very hot* after their lamp has been powered up for a few minutes. In a box with their vents partially blocked, and dry hay all around—these lights could start an unwanted *fire* onstage. There are several things you can do to reduce the chances of an embarrassing and dangerous accident: first, wrap the instrument in the manger with flame-proofed fabric between it and the hay. Second, you can make sure that this instrument is not powered up for more than a few minutes at any time. If it doesn't have time to heat up, it won't be a problem.

The Gifts of the Magi

One of the many interesting and nonbiblical traditions that has arisen around the Christ story is that there were *three* magi (astrologers, wise men, whatever you call them). Matthew, in fact, says nothing of the kind, only that they brought three *kinds of gifts*.[3] But tradition has taken hold, and so your Christmas pageant will very likely feature three people, each carrying a different box. But what should these boxes look like?

Perhaps they should not all be boxes. The gifts are gold, frankincense, and myrrh—and it is entirely suitable for the gold to be coins in a large velvet sack or pouch, the incense in a redecorated metal box (a brass incense burner of the kind often seen in furnishing-accessory stores), and the myrrh in an ornate clay jar.

One advantage of taking this approach is that the audience will be able to see at once that the gifts were all different, and even to make some guess as to which is which.

A more traditional approach is to have the magi carrying boxes that speak loudly of their origins. The wise men do, after all, come from "the East." So many Christmas shows will include props that look like the box pictured at left.

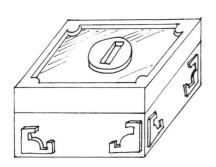

One way of making these is to build or purchase wooden jewelry boxes, adding the Oriental character shapes with a hardened clay such as Sculpey.[4] Then all visible surfaces of the box (inside and out!) are covered with gold foil such as that used in adding gold accents to picture frames.[5]

Campfires and Braziers

If you're staging a Christmas drama, the shepherds "abiding in the field" may need to have a campfire going—and if it's an Easter drama you're working on, you may need a fire for Peter's denial of Jesus.[6]

The problems of having a real fire onstage may be obvious, but for the sake of clarity I'll spell them out anyway. First, they are hard to start on cue. Second, they produce smoke. Third, they can get out of control and injure people and property.[7] Finally, anything with a fire in it tends to get hot—and is therefore very difficult to get offstage once the scene is over. But apart from these objections, the best way to represent a fire is with a fire.

3. In Matthew 2:1-12.

4. I'm a big fan of this modeling compound. Sculpey is more expensive than most other clays, but it is extremely easy to work with—and best of all, it can be hardened thoroughly in a conventional oven at temperatures as low as 250°! And you can even add pieces to a Sculpey creation that has already been hardened, bake it again, and then seamlessly paint the finished product. It can be found at most craft and hobby stores.

5. Available in most craft shops. The foil is extremely thin and delicate; it takes some practice before it can be handled properly. After it is glued down it should be coated with a glaze or varnish to keep it from flaking off.

6. The whole thing gets started because Peter tries to get close to the fire—at least that's how it happens in John 18:18-27.

7. One of the momentous events in the history of the theatre was when a stage fire got out of control during an early performance of Shakespeare's *Henry VIII*. The resulting blaze completely burned down the world-famous Globe Theatre. Let that be a lesson.

But let's assume you plan to simulate one. This could be considered a special effect—but I've grouped it into this part of the book because the fires I will describe can be handled like any other prop.

Patterns of Light. One method is to construct a self-contained unit that includes a lighting instrument and a small, slow-rotation motor, both of which can be controlled from offstage. The instrument is set into a brazier (basically a shallow pot) or into a bundles of sticks that have been wired together to hold their shape.

Alongside the lighting instrument, the motor should be attached to the nearest solid surface so its shaft reaches just above the lens of the instrument. A disk of thin metal (or foil-covered cardboard) is fitted onto the shaft. Random shapes are cut into the disk like so:

Orange, red, and amber gel[8] is taped to the top of the disk (the side away from the lamp) with gaffer's tape.[9] Now, when the disk rotates and the light shines through its odd-shaped holes, your actors should be illuminated in the odd flashes we associate with a crackling fire.

The trick described above will only work, however, if the audience's sight line is below the actors—that is, if they can't see into the top of the "campfire" or the brazier. But how can you create an onstage fire in an arena where the audience is looking down onto the stage?

Glowing Coals. I suggest you employ the effect of glowing embers instead of actual flames.[10] This can be done with a very similar setup to the one just described, only with a solid top instead of an open one. This solid top would be made of cast resin, transparent enough to allow light to shine through, but shaped like the outer surface of a burning pile of coals.

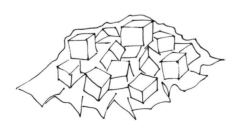

Casting resin is not as difficult as you might think. First you'll need to make a mold—I used a pile of discarded building-blocks.[11] Over these I laid a sheet of household plastic wrap. Then I poured about five pounds of plaster of paris over the whole mess. Once that hardened, I turned it over and pulled out the blocks and the plastic wrap. Voilà!—a negative image of a pile of roughly cube-shaped *somethings*.

Into this mold you'll now need to paint a *resin separator*. This is basi-

8. Colored transparent plastic, the mainstay of theatrical lighting. See the Appendix for sources.

9. Everywhere except show business, this is called duct tape.

10. It would be possible to create a self-contained unit that burned with real fire. It could include a propane-gas tank, a lighter, and a nozzle for spreading the jets of flame—but for a relatively minor effect in the production, this is a great deal of work. Reference the story I mentioned earlier, about the "water into wine" jug I once made. It's easy to get carried away with this props and effects stuff.

11. If you looked closely at the end product, you could still see some letters of the alphabet and things like that.

cally a chemical that keeps the resin from bonding to the mold so you can't get it back out! The separator is usually sold with the resin.

Now you're ready to pour in the clear resin. You'll want to use one that dries the hardest and the fastest, and remains resistant to extremes of temperature.[12] Pour some of this into the mold—just enough that when you "slosh" the mold around the resin paints the inside walls of the mold but does not gather into any puddles. Let the resin harden completely. You may need to repeat this several times, building up thicker and thicker resin in the mold. As usual, trial and error will give you the best results.

Once this is thoroughly dried, you can pull it out of the mold. You may have to break the plaster in the process. But once it's out, you should have a plastic shell that looks something like a pile of coals. Spray the inside of this with red-orange paint.[13]

This can be fitted into a contrivance like the ones described earlier, the "campfire" or the brazier. The plastic shell would go in like this:

Any bright light source will now give a fairly good impression of red-hot embers. If the power level of the lighting instrument under the shell is artfully raised and lowered throughout the scene, the embers will take on that "pulsing glow" familiar to anyone who has watched a large fire slowly burn itself out.

The final touch of realism is to fill the depressed areas of the plastic shell with some kind of gray powder. Why not use real ashes?

Jugs and Jars, Pots and Plates

A common stereotype of crowd scenes in biblical dramas is that everyone carries an earthen jar, whether he or she needs one or not, just because it "looks period." Even if your director has resisted this temptation, you may need a lot of earthenware to realistically create the world of first-century Judea. Happily, a red clay pot is basically a red clay pot, and always has been—so it's possible to go to your local garden-supply shop and find a pot that would be almost identical to one carried by the Samaritan woman when she visited the well.[14]

Note that I say "almost." Modern pottery is mostly made on or by machines—and so have perfectly formed shapes, clean edges, and uniform thicknesses. Crockery made by hand will not be so regular, so mechanical. If it's period authenticity that you're after in your props, then you may want to make your pots yourself.

12. See the Appendix for sources.

13. Your nearby hobby store should have special transparent paints that can be sprayed or brushed on. See the Appendix for one manufacturer of this kind of paint.

14. Described only in John 4:4-42.

45

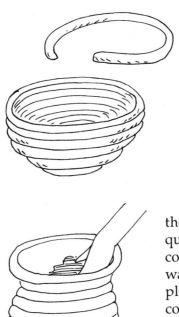

One of the simplest methods for doing this will be familiar to many kindergarten children: the "layers of coils" approach. This is simply building up your pottery in sections by rolling thin "snakes" of clay and then connecting them into circles that are stacked one on top of the other. Adhesion between the coils is attained by gently pressing each layer onto the one below it. With most clays, wetting each coil will help it to stick to any other clay it touches.

Once the desired shape has been built up, the entire pot is baked in the kiln or oven required by the kind of clay you have used. The coils can be blended into each other to give the walls of the pot added strength, but many people prefer the "ribbed" texture of the layered coils. One compromise is to carefully blend the coils together on the inside of the pot only. Of course this will only work if you have left an opening larger than your arm.

But what should these jugs and jars look like? There are many possibilities. For example, all of these shapes have been found in archaeological excavations of the ancient Middle East, so reproducing them will keep your pottery historically accurate:

Two of the simplest things you can make to lend authenticity to Bible drama are cups and lamps. Cups can be built up in layers as described above, but also by simply rolling a ball of clay and then digging a hole into the middle. The resulting irregular shape is a close match to cups found in many ancient dwellings.

Lamps are a little more complex, but only slightly. The kinds of oil lamps used in the time of Christ were basically flattened, roundish blobs of clay

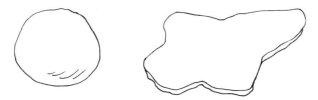

with the sides pinched up into a triangular cup with a guarded lip on one end. This "cup" is filled with oil and the "spout" end carefully touched to a flame.

If you've never lit a lamp of this kind before, it may take some practice—and as always when dealing with fire and flammable liquids, exercise all possible precautions. Keep a fire extinguisher handy. You may find that you will have to make several versions of the lamp before you get the shape of the spout just right.

Rocks, Both Large and Small

Since so much of the Christ story takes place outdoors, you may find you have to construct props or set pieces that convey to the audience the image of the rocky terrain of the Middle East. One classic picture that many directors like to make is of Jesus praying in Gethsemane, his body draped over a large stone so his face will stay up where the audience can see him. But dragging a real boulder onstage and off just for this scene is probably impractical. So a realistic fake stone must be created instead.[15]

Stones to Stand On. Depending on the size and weight of the stone you plan to build—and how much weight it must be able to hold—you may be able to construct the rock out of Polyfoam.

Polyfoam is commonly used in household insulation and can be purchased from a supplier of home building materials. It can be cut into almost any shape, glued together with an adhesive such as Liquid Nails, can be painted with latex paints (*not* spray enamels—they will eat the foam!) and are lightweight but very strong. Textures and patterns can be cut into the foam with anything raised to a high temperature: a soldering iron, a woodburner, a butane torch.

Since the foam is usually sold in sheets, you may have to lightly glue several together to get the bulk you need, and then carve the stone out of the block you've made.

Be extremely careful when cutting Polyfoam! Many varieties release a *poisonous gas* when burned—so if you do any cutting or modeling with a torch, soldering iron, or similar device, be sure to do so *outdoors* and while

15. For another discussion of fake stones for the stage, see the "Resurrection" section in Part One of this book.

47

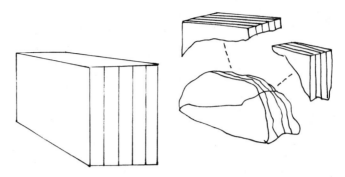

16. Ask me how I know.

17. Available in small and medium quantities from craft and hobby stores. If you want to buy a larger quantity of PlasterCraft, contact a medical equipment supplier.

wearing a mask over your nose and mouth. If you try to carve this material with a hot iron of some kind while indoors, you are liable to end up on the floor, unconscious—or worse.[16]

You may also get good results using PlasterCraft, the material doctors use to set broken bones. It's basically a roll of gauze, but the entire length has been impregnated with dry plaster.[17] So you just cut off as much as you can handle, wet it lightly—then apply and let dry. Very soon you will have a hard plaster shell where a moment before there was a soggy rag. If your rocks do not have to bear any weight, PlasterCraft is the perfect material for making the exterior surface of the stones. And if you build a platform that will support an actor, you can use PlasterCraft to blend the load-bearing section with any parts of the rock that have been constructed of wire, cardboard, or some other lightweight structure.

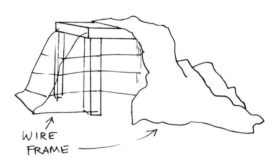

WIRE
FRAME

Another method you may want to consider is the use of *blown fiberglass.* This is probably the most expensive option but can also be the most effective. The process was developed for the house-building industry; a giant machine forces liquidized fiberglass into the cracks, crannies, and crevices of walls, quickly hardening into a dense, rigid mass that blocks the escape of air throughout the home where it has been applied. A local building contractor can tell you how to get the services of a fiberglass-spraying expert. You may have some trouble convincing him or her that you want this stuff sprayed all over your church's backyard, but promise them they won't be held responsible for the mess and they should agree to it.

Build up your framework according to the set design and the action the director plans. For example, will anyone stand on this rock once it is completed? If so, your "skeleton" should include a platform that would support the actor fully. From this you should extend a coating of mesh or paper everywhere that you wish to simulate a stone's surface. The fiberglass will be sprayed on top of this underpinning and will generally take the shape of whatever you've built underneath. The spray fiberglass will stick to any surface with holes smaller than about one-half inch, so any sort of screen or fencing with sufficiently small holes will do nicely.

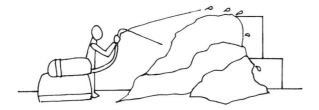

Once the fiberglass has hardened, it can be painted with spray paints (or with brushes, for that matter, but the surface is so lumpy it would take a long, long time) and should still be light enough to be easily carried back into your theatre.

Throwing Stones. If you are enacting any of the executions-by-stoning in the Bible, then you will need rocks that you can safely throw at an actor. Now, as I've mentioned before, it's never perfectly safe to hit anybody with anything, but there *are* substances that are much safer than others. Naturally your rocks will need to be specially constructed out of one of these relatively harmless materials.

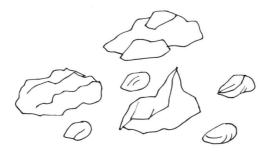

What about sponge rubber, that wonderful bunch of chemicals that has solved so many of our other special effects and props problems? It can be painted to look exactly like rock and will certainly be "safe" to throw at an actor. Foam has only one real drawback, and if you're trying to depict a stoning, it's a major one: it *bounces*. Even the dense, heavy Polyfoam compounds will reveal themselves to be mostly air when they are not perfectly at rest.[18]

So what looks like a rock, handles like a rock, but can be thrown at an actor with relative safety—and will not bounce? Beanbags.

You read that right: beanbags. A sack or pouch containing any kind of small, dried beans will work—in fact I suggest birdseed instead of actual beans. Just pour a few cups of the beans or seeds into a plastic bag and tape it into a ball.

Now cover this with a piece of light-but-strong cloth such as muslin or gabardine. Stitch this together firmly. Either sew it completely up like a

18. In the "Friday's Child" episode of the original *Star Trek* series there is a particularly embarrassing effects sequence in which a group of people get caught in an avalanche of obviously foam-rubber boulders. Even the miracles-on-a-shoestring effects team for that show failed to make these rocks look convincing. So if you ever consider building rocks out of foam, watch this episode before you make your decision.

baseball, or if you're short on time (and don't have a dozen people on hand who can sew) put a few stitches in and paint the whole rock with liquid latex or a white glue such as Elmer's Glue-All. Allow this to dry, then add another coat. Repeat as many times as you think is needed. Then, when the rock is thoroughly dry, paint it with a latex paint. Take care to dab the pigment on instead of brushing—you'll get a more realistic blend of colors.[19]

You should make these in all different sizes, since they're supposed to be naturally occurring stones that your mob has found lying around. Just be sure to keep them small enough that they will not be able to droop.

19. I have also heard of the bags beings held together with the self-adhesive stretchable material made by Ace Bandage. This sounds like it would probably work very well, and the bandage should take the paint at least as well as the gabardine or muslin.

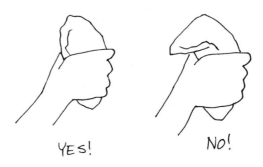

YES!   NO!

This will be a dead giveaway that the actor is holding something besides a real rock.

Will they *sound* like real rocks hitting a person? Well, I've never witnessed a real stoning, but I think this sound must be pretty close—especially if both the stoners and the stonee are all screaming at the tops of their voices. This is not only perfectly natural but will conceal whatever un-rock-like noise the beanbags do make.

Swords

Another danger zone. As with rocks and fires, there's just no such thing as a perfectly safe stage sword. No matter what you make it out of, it's still shaped like a sword, and it's the *shape* that makes a sword dangerous in the first place. So keeping all of that in mind, how can you make swords for your soldiers and zealots in a drama of the first century?

First of all, consider what the swords of the day were like. Since the Roman Empire was effectively in military control of the entire world, weapons of all peoples tended to be patterned after those carried by the centurions and their comrades. But the Roman sword is basically a thrusting weapon, not a cutting blade—so how could Simon Peter have used one to cut off Malchus's ear?[20]

20. See the discussion of this in Part One of this book.

The fact is, what Simon Peter probably had was really more of a knife than a sword—and that gives us an idea of the two basic types of blades you would have seen back then:

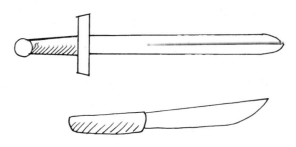

Temple Guards and the soldiers of Herod could quite possibly have carried swords a bit more like their previous conquerors, the Greeks.

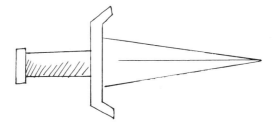

As you can see, all of these are basically flat pieces of metal with a simple handle screwed on. And that's really the best way to make them, especially if you are skilled at working with metals. Do *not* sharpen the edges! The audience can't see if the blade has a sharpened edge or not, and it's only asking for trouble if you make one.[21]

A less expensive and somewhat safer method is to carve the blades out of wood or Masonite and then cover the blade with the chrome tape used by auto detailers. Many auto-supply stores now carry small rolls of this highly reflective tape, usually about one inch wide. If kept smooth, the tape looks uncannily like polished steel (unlike aluminum foil, the hallmark of the cheap-looking theatrical blade). Just layer the strips across the blade lengthwise, being careful to keep the edges as neat as possible to help them appear invisible.

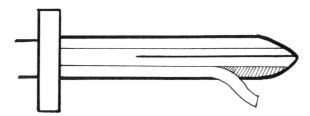

You may be pleasantly surprised at how effective this simple trick can be.

Palm Branches

A truly ambitious passion play might include the construction of authentic trees of the Middle East, complete with palm leaves. But even the poorest of Easter dramas will probably include the Triumphant Entry, and for that you will certainly need recognizable branches.[22] And not all of us live in Florida or California. So how to get palms onto the stage?

Once when I was a volunteer helper for our church's Vacation Bible School I was asked to make some palm leaves according to a pattern given by the VBS materials we had purchased. I was dubious; the description given seemed *too easy*. But I dutifully did as I was told—and was very pleased with the result! So I want to pass this trick on to you just as it was taught to me.

Paper bags. Yes, the ordinary brown kind you sometimes get at the grocery store. If you cut along their folded seams, you can flatten them out in several ways. Here are the two that will be useful to you in making palm leaves:

21. This may sound like an obvious precaution, but I have been amazed at how many Bible epics are staged with soldiers running around carrying real, metal, sharpened knives.

22. Once again, it depends on which Gospel your script is based upon. Matthew 21:8 tells us the crowd cut "branches from the trees," but some translations of Mark 11:8 says they were cut out of the fields. Luke 19 mentions only the clothes that people put onto the road ahead of Jesus. But John 12:13—good old John—tells us expressly that the crowd carried "the branches of palm trees." And such was apparently the custom.

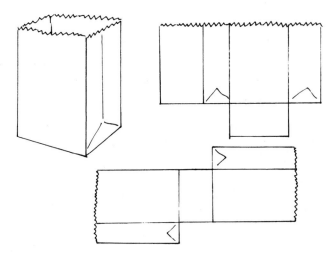

Now double these over and cut the leaves out in one of these shapes:

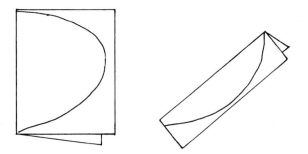

Still doubled, "fringe" the edges of the leaves like this:

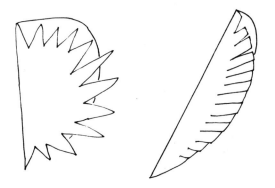

One side of this will probably have some printing on it. Spray-paint this side dark green. (It may take several coats—grocery stores like to print their bags with vivid *red* ink! Be sure to let the paint dry thoroughly between coats.) Leave the other side alone—it's the perfect color already.

While this is drying, cut another bag apart and make strips about

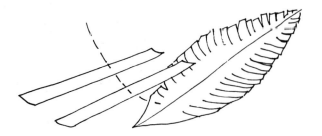

two inches wide. Double these and glue the two sides together. For a sturdier leaf, add something rigid inside, such as a stick or a piece of wire.

Now you can trim one end so it comes to a point—and glue it right along the center fold of the leaf on the "natural color" side. For added strength, you may want to use tan-colored packing tape. Even though it's very glossy, if you apply it neatly and trim the end to a point, it will look like the shiny part of the stalk.

And that's it! Now you just have to do it all 50 more times.

Animals (Well, Sort Of)

Few Christmas pageants can afford to have live sheep, donkeys, cows, and the like onstage. Add to this the tradition that the magi arrived on camels, and you have an interesting dilemma on your hands: how to represent the animals that figure so prominently in the story?

I have seen this done very effectively with a design trick that I admit will not work for every production. But some clever variation of it probably will. I leave that to your imagination. The idea is to make silhouettes of the animals out of plywood and prop them up parallel to the audience.

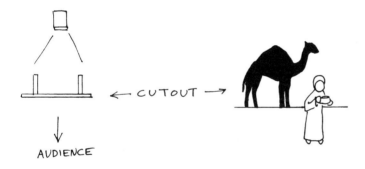

Lit from behind, they become still, silent parts of the scenery and yet are a constant reminder that the animals are very much a part of the story.

The drawings on the following pages are scaled onto a standard 4 x 8 sheet of plywood. The easiest way to get them from the page to the piece

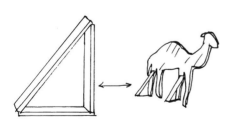

of wood is to copy the drawing onto a transparency, then use an overhead projector to create an image on the wood that can be traced with a Magic Marker. Then a jigsaw will do the rest.

The stands ("jacks," we call them in the theatre) are very simple pieces of 2 x 4 lumber, as seen at left.

Once the figures have been cut and attached to their stands, the whole assembly should be painted *matte* black. Be careful not to use *gloss* black paint by mistake; it will make the silhouettes slightly reflective, reminding the audience that these are not backlit animals but two-dimensional cutouts.

Advanced Project: The Head of John the Baptist

Undoubtedly the most difficult prop I've ever made for an Easter drama was the severed head of John the Baptist. Making such a thing the way we did required a wide variety of skills, expensive materials, and quite a lot of patience. But if you're staging a passion play and the script recounts the whole ugly incident of the beheading of John,[23] the final effect of a well-made prop just might be worth it.

As tempting as it might be to use a wig block with a face painted on it or a dimestore face mask that doesn't even have eyeballs,[24] by far the most effective "severed head" is going to be based on the real head of the actor who will portray John. This means you'll be making a life cast, a difficult and even potentially dangerous project for which you will want to get several volunteers to help. Most of all, you'll need the willing cooperation of the actor who is going to have his face completely covered for about half an hour with thick dental alginate and several inches of plaster.

A full explanation of making life casts is too complex for this book, so if you're not already an expert on this, please consult the Appendix for specialized sources on this topic. But the idea is to inject a liquid-rubber compound called *foam latex* into the finished mold. Foam latex expands and hardens when heated and dried, so it goes from a watery mess to looking and feeling very much like human flesh.

The result will be a humanlike head that at this point should resemble the actor it was modeled after, especially after it has been painted with colors that closely match the makeup he'll wear in the show.

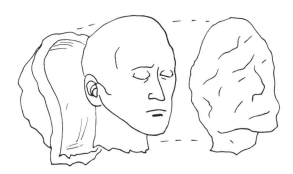

We cut some of the foam from the neck of this prop so it would rest properly when carried on a platter. Since this left a ragged edge where the neck used to be, we took advantage of the opportunity to weight the base of the head by sticking heavy pieces of metal into the soft foam inside. Then we painted over the base of the head with liquid latex, allowing several coats to dry before going on to any other step.

We were fortunate where the *hair* for this drama's John the Baptist was concerned because he wore a thick black wig onstage. So we simply bought an identical wig and literally sewed it onto the latex head.[25] We were also lucky that the actor had thick black eyebrows and eyelashes—these we painted onto the latex head with ordinary black latex paint.

26. We knew we had an effective prop after the actor's girlfriend happened to come into the prop shop one day. She almost fainted when she saw, resting casually on a table littered with paint cans and power tools, her boyfriend's head.

27. Such as the ear that Simon Peter cuts off at Gethsemane, or even false hands for the Crucifixion. The use of these props is discussed in Part One of this book.

We experimented at length with the colors in the face, trying to get as close a match to the actor's own complexion as possible. As usual, trial and error did the trick.[26]

Specific Body Parts

If your script calls for other body parts,[27] a simplified version of this process will do the trick. Simply pour the alginate over the part to be copied, backing it with plaster if necessary. Once this has set, remove it carefully from the actor and paint in layer after layer of liquid latex. (You can force each layer dry with a hair dryer, but be patient; it's going to take a long time no matter what you do.)

Now get some makeup setting powder or talcum powder and keep it nearby—when you peel the latex piece out of the mold you'll need to dab the powder onto the latex to keep the fresh rubber from sticking to itself. Meanwhile, gently poke at the latex with a pencil-point to see it's fully dried. It should have changed colors as it set, but even after that it still has some "thickening" to do. When the latex seems thick enough to survive the rigors of performance, peel it cautiously out of the mold, brushing powder onto every freshly exposed surface of the latex.

Trim the excess off and paint the finished piece to match the actor's makeup. Looks lifelike, doesn't it? Take some time now to marvel over the complexity of God's creation.

That's it for props. But before you're left to your own devices, I'd like to share a few last thoughts on some effects that are not quite effects . . . and some props that are not quite props.

Part Three
Assorted Miracles

Since Jesus taught us to go the extra mile, I don't want to simply leave you after covering only the special effects and props promised by the title of this book. There are still a few things you may want to consider as you approach the effects and props for your biblical drama.

Sound

Effects and props must fool the eye, but it's easy to forget that they must fool the ear as well. A prop that looks right but sounds wrong will be well-remembered by your audience—and they'll remember it with a snicker.[1] Special effects are perhaps even more reliant than props on *sound* to fool the audience.

Take for example the Crucifixion. Suppose you have decided to deal with the driving of the nails by having the action unseen by the audience, either in a blackout or with an actor in front of the actual nail-driving. Both of these approaches will require the *sound* of the nails being driven. The sound could be produced by someone "live," but the person would naturally have to be offstage and out of range of the audience's vision, probably muffling the sound. So the best alternative is probably a prerecorded sound.

Back in the so-called "good old days" we used to record these kinds of sound cues on reel-to-reel magnetic tape and then paint a white mark onto the exact point on the tape where each sound began. Then in performance, we would cue the tape player up by running the reels silently until one of the white spots approached the machine's "play" head. Then at the appropriate moment, we would punch the "play" button and hope that the white spot we had stopped on was in fact the correct one.[2]

Today we are fortunate to have the CD—the compact disc. Gone is the visual cuing; a digital readout on your player will pinpoint the beginning of each sound or music cue you want to use. And because the mechanism inside the player is electronic and not mechanical, gone also is the "clunk" that used to accompany every sound cue done the old-fashioned way. Now you just press a button and your sound effect pours forth instantly and with no unwanted noise.

There are plenty of sound effects CDs on the market. (Check your favorite general-interest record store in the section marked "Spoken Word" —it's usually the closest category to "Sound Effects" that a music store is liable to have.) But biblical dramas have special needs, and most effects CDs are loaded with exclusively 20th-century noises.

To your rescue comes a compact disc from Lillenas titled *Sound Effects for Seasonal Productions*.[3] There are few passion plays that will require a sound effect that is *not* on this disc. Whether you need the sound of donkey's hooves on a stone road, an earthquake, or the hammering of those nails—it's all in this collection, along with musical "bridges" to cover scene changes, accompany marching soldiers, or to lend atmosphere to the Passover meal.

1. I once outfitted the villain in a murder mystery with a plastic handgun, which at one point in the show he accidentally dropped—producing a distinctly hollow "clack" instead of the "thud" you might expect. The audience laughed out loud during the supposedly thrilling climax of the play. And that was nobody's fault but my own.

2. I don't mean to make fun of this; if you have a special sound or music cue that needs to be recorded and played back, this is still probably the best way to do it.

3. See the Appendix for more details.

Sleight of Hand

It has been said in many passion plays over the years that the great thing about period costumes for first-century Judea is that they offer plenty of places to hide things. And it's true; many miracles have seemingly been worked onstage because the actors had things tucked invisibly up their sleeves.

Now, add to that some education in prestidigitation—sleight of hand—for your actors, and the audience can be truly amazed.

One variety of such tricks that I've mentioned several times in this book is "palming." There's nothing mysterious about palming; it's just the skill of keeping something in your hand in such a way that you don't appear to be holding anything at all. There are a variety of ways of doing this, and the only rule is "do whatever works best."[4] Using the example from Part One of this book in which Simon Peter palms the ear he will later supposedly cut from Malchus's head, any of these methods should work well:

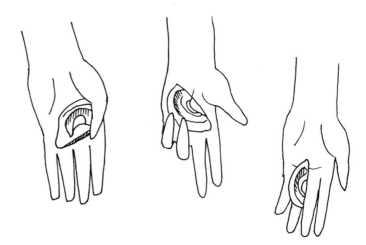

Have your actors practice and practice this until they feel completely relaxed and natural. One of the quickest ways for them to give themselves away while palming something is to look uncomfortable. If the actor does not appear exactly as he ordinarily would, a tiny doubt will begin to grow in the audience's mind.[5]

Fighting and Other Mayhem

The Christ story is a violent tale. Even if the only aggressive act in the story was the Crucifixion, that would be more than enough. But there are in fact several events in the tale that may require the actors to represent people fighting, rioting, or otherwise appearing to injure each other. This is close enough to being a "special effect" that I thought I should mention it briefly here.

Take for example the horrible part of the Christmas story in which Herod orders the slaughter of the children.[6] We must assume that the soldiers met with some resistance from the fathers and mothers of these babies. So if your seasonal drama calls for this battle to be shown onstage, how will you go about it? The answer: *very carefully.*[7]

The same holds true for the cleansing of the Temple or any other scene of crowd violence in your show. Your director needs to deal with these portions of the show with extreme care, making certain that every

4. And although no book can teach this—only hours of practice—I recommend the sources described in the Appendix.

5. I believe we can all somehow sense these things—and when we're watching plays we tend to naturally zero in on "how the trick is done."

6. Matthew 2:16-18.

7. But see the 1961 film *King of Kings* for a particularly effective treatment of this incident, in which there is no actual fighting seen—mostly the anguish of the mothers whose children are being killed. You may want to consider handling the scene in this way.

single person onstage knows where to be and what to be doing every single instant of the fighting. My motto for choreographing stage fights is: "Don't fight—*dance.*" Because it isn't really a fight, of course—it's a dance that *looks* like a fight, a step-by-step preplanned series of movements that will simulate people doing injury to each other. Start very, very slowly and gradually, over the course of several rehearsals, increase the speed until the fight is happening in realistic motion—and every person onstage is sticking to their blocking every second of the way.[8]

For the sake of realism, encourage the actors in the fight to remember Newton's third law of motion: "Every action has an equal and opposite reaction." Fight scenes in movies and on TV very often show someone punching someone else without really hurting either person. This is simply not how it works; slinging your fist into someone's jawbone hurts both fist and jawbone. When you push someone, the person should fall backward. When two swords clash together, the impact is sorely felt in the arms of both swordsmen. Very often actors seem to forget that when they are on the receiving end of a stage punch, it is their job to fall down.[9]

Animals (Live Ones)

In Part Two of this book we discussed one way of creating the *illusion* of animals onstage. But suppose you are staging a highly realistic Easter drama. Can you present an authentic, canonical Triumphant Entry without a donkey colt? The animal plays an important part in all of the scriptural accounts,[10] so you can't just wish the poor beast away.

Live animals add another dimension to a biblical drama that simply can't be simulated or replaced. They remind of us how agrarian the world of the first century was, and of the degree to which the men and women of the Bible relied on various animals in their daily lives. And they can be used to make powerful visual statements; it is one thing to show five Roman soldiers threatening a group of five Jewish zealots—but put all the Romans on horseback and leave the Jews on foot, and you have an entirely new dynamic of power and authority.

But animals do also pose many problems. First, they will probably require someone whose sole job is to tend the animals. Second, they do not follow stage directions very well. Finally, they do have an unfortunate tendency to relieve themselves onstage,[11] which if nothing else will attract attention away from the intended focus of the scene.

So are live animals in your production worth the effort? Perhaps the best answer to this question is: it all depends. If your performances will take place outdoors and you have the budget and staff to do it properly, then by all means do it. But don't forget to do the following first:

8. As with palming, practice makes perfect and you really can't learn this from simply reading a book. Still, I encourage you to study the books on stage combat and on direction, described in the Appendix.

9. One reason for this is that some people wish to appear invulnerable onstage. So an actor throws a stage-punch at them—which is intended to look like a mighty blow—and the recipient of the punch enjoys looking as if that didn't hurt him. But in fact it only makes the punch look faked—which it was.

10. In Matthew 21:1-9, Mark 11:1-10, and Luke 19:28-40. In John's Gospel it looks like we're going to get out of needing a colt—but then John 12:14-15 sneaks up and surprises us.

11. I have heard of a passion play in which Pilate rode in on a beautiful horse—which then bucked him off, backed its rear over him and . . . well, you can guess the rest. More than one person observed that the horse seemed to share the opinion of Pilate held by many Christians.

1. Make sure you can provide everything they will need to eat.

2. Make sure there is safe and reliable transportation between the stage and wherever the animals are sheltered.

3. Arrange for a veterinarian to be on call—or actually present—throughout the run of your show.

4. Make sure the animals will be kept in a place where there is absolutely no chance of their hurting anyone should they be frightened or, still worse, injured.[12]

If your production will be staged indoors, you must take all of the steps listed above plus the following:

1. Find out the exact health and safety regulations concerning animals on your premises. If it's prohibited, then stop right there.

2. Coordinate with the building's maintenance crew. There *will* be special cleaning to be done once the show is over, and it can be minimized with precautions that the maintenance experts can recommend.

But suppose you don't plan to use live animals. What *do* you do about, say, the Triumphant Entry?

My best advice would be to have large parts of the action take place offstage. For example, in the case of the Triumphant Entry, you could stage the scene so that what the audience sees is the crowd anticipating Jesus' arrival.

Then from offstage (on a recording) we would hear the sound of Jesus' colt on the stone streets of Jerusalem.[13] Ad-libs in the onstage crowd would do the rest. "Will He stop here? Or will He just ride by? No, wait—He's climbing down! He's coming this way!" And then Jesus would enter on foot.

Controlling Fog and Smoke

In Part One of this book the use of fog and fog machines was briefly discussed. Another few words on the subject are probably needed.

The excellent machines currently available for producing vapor clouds onstage are virtual miracle workers: inexpensive to rent, easy to control, and generally very quiet. But controlling the vapor does pose some challenges. It's so easy to get a stream of clouds emanating from one of the machines that you may be tempted to forget how hard it is to get the fog to go away again. So be careful not to plan to fill the stage up with smoke or fog and expect to have the next scene performed in clear air.

Time is also a factor to consider if you want to have a very high volume of fog appear at once. Basically the machines are pumps with spray-nozzles through which the vapor is scattered, and the harder you pump, the greater the volume—both of fog and *noise*. I have seen many plays in which a character was supposed to appear in a huge cloud of smoke—a

12. This may sound like a remote possibility, but it's the sort of thing you don't want to have happen even once.

13. See the Appendix for a compact disc containing this sound effect.

genie from Aladdin's lamp or some such—and the "magical" entry was preceded by a noise that sounded like an approaching locomotive.

But I have also seen an ingenious solution to this problem: a dry-cleaning bag, the clear plastic sheaths that are put over clean clothes for the customer to carry home. Stagehands held one of these bags over the nozzle of the fog machine a minute or so before the "magical entrance"—pumped the bag full of fog—then at the appropriate moment, one stagehand held the mouth of the bag open while another pushed the closed end straight through the mouth. The fog that had been held in the bag came rolling out in one giant cloud.

The catch—you knew there had to be one—is timing. The fog breaks down in the bag very quickly, settling into nothingness. And if you try to force the bag full just before the cue, you'll have to pump hard and make that awful racket—the problem you were trying to avoid in the first place. But with practice you *can* time this out so that it works. It just takes time.

One church's Easter pageant called for a fog bank that spread out over a wide area very quickly, and the solution they used was to basically build a simple sprinkler system, such as you might use in your front yard. The fog machine was hooked up just as the water would be, and at the appropriate moment the fog was pumped through—and crept out onto the stage in several places at once.

This brilliant solution to a puzzling problem was related to me at one of Lillenas's Drama in the Church Workshops by someone who went on to say that the man who saved the day installed sprinkler systems for a living. He had thought he had nothing to contribute to the church's drama ministry. This is a powerful example of how wide a variety of gifts are needed to put on a good Christmas or Easter drama. It also demonstrates the importance of . . .

Making the Best Use of What You Have

This is the last aspect of creating effects and props that I wanted to discuss with you, and I have deliberately saved it for last because it just may be the most important.

The above story, about the man who installs sprinkler systems, is typical of discoveries made during virtually every play performed by a community theatre group or church drama program. There are many, many people in your church who probably think they have nothing to offer to something as "artsy" as the theatre. Later you may discover that they feel this way because they are "only" electrical contractors, or that they "only know how to sew," or that they "only" install fiberglass insulation.

On one level, it's simply good for you to discover untapped talent for your production. But I propose to you that this also illustrates something deeper and more important. Namely, that part of our mission in Christian drama is to continually experience each person we meet in a new way: not seeing people merely for what they *are* (or what we perceive them to be), but for what they are *capable of becoming*. That building contractor in your congregation who rarely attends Sunday services may be drifting away from the faith . . . and waiting for someone in the church community to ask for his help on a complex problem with your stage's construction.

This attitude extends to inanimate objects as well. For example, my effects work has often called for hand pumps—rubber squeeze-bulbs—which I have sometimes had great difficulty in finding. Then one day I was in a drugstore and happened to look at a device for spraying medicinal drops into a baby's nose. Part of this contraption was exactly the kind of squeeze-bulb I needed. I saw the nose-sprayer not as what it *was*, but as what it was *capable of becoming*.

I believe we have much cause to rejoice in the fact that God sees *us* this way.[14] And I believe He wants us to view our world—and especially each other—in the same manner. In fact, I'd guess that if the world of effects and props is the place where you practice thinking this way, then you will be a blessing to every production, and God will be glorified—onstage and off.

14. This belief forms the basis of the play *A Rock and a Hard Place,* which I wrote with my friend Robert Montgomery. Lillenas item MP-750.

Appendix:
How to Find Stuff

This is a fairly comprehensive listing of things you may need for your show. And many of the books listed in this appendix include detailed lists of sources for other books and materials—so the possibilities are endless!

Materials

General Sources

The Debbies Book. Depending on who you ask, it's either *Debbie's Book* or *The Debbies Book,* but whatever you call it, drop what you're doing and get one. Its advertising claims it is "The Bible to the Entertainment Industry" and *"The Source Book for Prop and Set Dressing."* And in fact, these are not exaggerations. The brainchild of Deborah Ann Hemela, *Debbie's Book* is really just a collection of addresses and phone numbers, paid for by the businesses represented—just like the yellow pages. But in this book, the advertisers are Hollywood effects and props houses, costumers, makeup specialty dealers, machine shops, wholesale fabric merchants, importers, armorers. In short, if the businesses represented in *Debbie's Book* don't have what you're looking for, you probably need to look for something else.

Write to *Debbie's Book* at P.O. Box 40968, Pasadena, CA 91114, or call 818-798-7968. The fax number is 818-798-5563.

Norcostco. For many theatrical designers, Norcostco is the ultimate one-stop shopping outlet. With branches in every region of the continental U.S., they carry lighting and sound equipment, fog machines, mirror balls, gobos, wireless headset systems, modeling and casting compounds, stage makeup, wigs and beards, prop swords, and much more. On top of this they are one of the world's largest costume rental houses.

Main office: 3203 N. Hwy. 100, Minneapolis, MN 55422-2789. Call for their catalog: 612-533-2791.

Edmund Scientific. Prisms, mirrors, casting and modeling compounds, small motors and pumps, rubber tubing, luminous paints, tools for extremely fine work, fiber optics, lasers, and much more.

101 E. Gloucester Pike, Barrington, NJ 08007-1380. Call for their catalog: 609-573-6260.

Specific Sources

Alginate. Teledyne Dental, Getz Apatow Division, 1550 Green Leaf Ave., Elk Grove Village, IL 60007 (312-593-3334).

Casting Resin. Castin'Craft, c/o ETI, P.O. Box 365, Fields Landing, CA 95537.

Electrical Connectors. Try Angstrom Stage Lighting, 837 N. Cahuenga Blvd., Hollywood, CA 90038 (800-422-5744).

Fog and Fogging Machines. Norcostco; see above.

Gobos. American Light Company.

Gold Foil. Delta Technical Coatings, Whittier, CA 90601.

Lamps. Norcostco; see above.

Latex. Foam and Liquid forms, as well as the paints to match prostheses to makeup—all available from Alcone Company, 575 Eighth Ave., New York, NY 10018 (212-594-3980).

You may also want to try Ben Nye, Inc., 11571 Santa Monica Blvd., Los Angeles, CA 90025 (213-478-1558).

Flameproofing. Norcostco; see above.

Lighting Equipment. Norcostco; see above.

Connectors. (see Electrical Connectors)

Mirror Balls. Norcostco; see above.

Papier-mâché. Celluclay, Activa Products, P.O. Box 1296, Marshall, TX 75670-0023.

Plastic Tubing. Edmund Scientific; see above.

Resin. See Casting Resin.

ScotchLite. Call 3M Sales and Product Information for the outlet nearest you (1-800-364-3577).

Scrim. Norcostco; see above.

Sculpey (also Super Sculpey and Sculpey III). Polyform Products Co., Schiller Park, IL 60176.

Stage Blood. Kryolan Corporation. 14316 Victory Blvd., Van Nuys, CA 91401 (213-787-5054).

Stage Fog. Norcostco; see above.

Transparent Paints. Norcostco; see above.

Velour. Norcostco; see above.

Books and Recordings

I've included ISBN numbers whenever I was sure of them; your nearest bookseller should be able to track any book down once given that number. Happy hunting!

Building Special Props

There are two books that will very likely guide you through any special construction you'll ever need—and will do it with clear, simple instructions and vivid photographs. You just can't beat *The What, When, and Where of Theater Props* (1-55870-257-1) and *The Prop Builder's Molding and Casting Handbook* (1-55870-128-1), both by a remarkable artisan named Thurston James. Step-by-step guidance, profusely illustrated, on making an astounding variety of special props and decorations for your show. An amazing pair of books (actually, there is a third as well that deals with making masks).

The series was published by Betterway Books; as of this writing they can be reached at 800-289-0963.

To accurately re-create the world of, say, Ancient Rome or of the Egypt of the Pharaohs, your set designer, costume designer, and *you* will probably need reference materials on *ornamentation*. There are two definitive works on just what the fine details of ancient art and architecture, jewelry and jugs really looked like: The *Handbook of Ornament* by Franz Sales Meyer, and *The Styles of Ornament* by Alexander Speltz. Both have been printed by Dover Publications. *Styles* deals in extraordinary depth (and thousands of illustrations) with a wide variety of cultures ranging from Egypt to the Babylonians and up to the Early

Christian Era. *Handbook* gives examples from fewer cultures, but in great depth and detail of the main civilizations such as the Romans and Greeks.

Scenic and Lighting Design

Easy Scenery Design and Construction by Michael Shew. A clear and concise, step-by-step description of how to plan and build simple theatrical sets. A handy guidebook for novice and expert alike, and refreshingly upbeat thanks to Shew's cartoons and commentary. Lillenas Drama Resources item No. MP-511 (083-419-0605).

Scene Design and Stage Lighting by W. Oren Parker and Harvey K. Smith. One of the tried-and-true standard books on the subject. Holt, Rinehart, and Winston (03-020761-4).

Stage Scenery: Its Construction and Rigging by A. S. Gillette and J. Michael Gillette. A very clear and well-illustrated guide to the nuts and bolts of building things for the stage. Descriptions give enough detail for the beginner, enough challenge for the expert. Harper and Row (0-06-042332-3).

Theatrical Design and Production by J. Michael Gillette. Designed to be a university textbook, this book comes from Mayfield Publishing. If you decided to buy only one book on designing and building for the theatre, this should be the one. A bit hard to track down but well worth the chase, Gillette's book takes you through building scenery, hanging scrims, constructing special props, prosthetic makeup. It's astounding how much he's gotten between the two covers of this book, and without short-changing any one aspect of the art. A life-saver.

Drafting Scenery for Theatre, Film, and Television by Rich Rose. From Betterway Publications (1-55870-141-9). Do you have trouble making good drawings and plans from which to build things? If so, get this book. Rose explains everything—from keeping proportional scale in perspective to choosing the right kind of drawing table.

Special Painted Effects

Professional Painted Finishes by Ina Brosseau Marx. The ultimate book on painting the texture and color of stone work and woodgrains onto things that are not stones or wood. For example, Marx gives detailed instructions on how to create the effect of at least a dozen different kinds of marble. A beautiful book to look at it, it will be priceless in helping you paint the various artificial rocks you may create for your passion play. Published by Watson-Guptill (0-8230-4418-1).

Special Makeup Effects

Techniques of Three-Dimensional Makeup by Lee Baygan. A practical guidebook for any enthusiastic amateur with a gift for sculpting and painting, by NBC-TV's director of makeup. Absolutely essential if you plan to do elaborate prosthetics or a head of John the Baptist. Published by Watson-Guptill Publications (0-8230-5260-5).

Stage Makeup by Richard Corson. The ubiquitous text for the budding actor or makeup artist. Corson discusses prosthetics briefly but well, with many helpful photographs. This is an outstanding overview of all kinds of makeup for the stage (0-13-840512-3).

Directing and Planning a Production

What to Do with the Second Shepherd on the Left: Staging the Seasonal Musical by Deborah Craig-Claar. The most thorough-but-concise book I've ever seen on the process of getting a complex show from the page to the stage. Invaluable for directors, this book is also a fine introduction for designers and performers to the "big picture" of theatrical production. I'd be a big fan of this book even if it *didn't* come from Lillenas! Ask for item No. MP-671.

Producing and Directing Drama for the Church by Robert Rucker. A complete how-to for directors and producers who are beyond the "beginner" level and looking for greater challenges. Thorough, provocative, and well-written. Lillenas Drama Resource No. MP-681.

The Complete Play Production Handbook by Carl Allensworth. Allensworth almost tries to get too much into one book, but if you're starting a community theatre or church drama program, this book may be a very good place to begin your learning process. Harper and Row (0-06-015000-9).

Stage Combat

Combat Mime: A Nonviolent Approach to Stage Violence by J. D. Martinez. Easy-to-follow directions, profusely illustrated. Martinez is obviously a highly skilled teacher; he makes every aspect of this difficult skill perfectly clear—and so exciting that you may be tempted to tackle a script with plenty of fight scenes just so you can use all the tricks Martinez teaches. There are other books on stage combat, but none come close to this one.

Magic and Sleight of Hand

Magic with Coins and Bills by Bill Severn. There are thousands of how-to books on magic tricks (many of them by Bill Severn!) but this has the most concise description I've ever seen of easy methods of "palming" things (0-679-20380-X).

Music and Sound Effects

Sound Effects for Seasonal Productions. The complete, ready-to-play audio portion of your seasonal Bible drama, all on one easy-to-use CD. Seventy-five music bridge and sound effects cues, compiled, scored, and edited by Craig Paddock and Paul M. Miller. Lillenas Drama Resources item No. MU-9188T.

"Bible Times" Reference

Everyday Life in Bible Times. Part of the National Geographic Society's "Stories of Man" series. Beautiful, concise, well-researched, and utterly comprehensive. Originally published in 1967; if this is out of print, perhaps your local library has this on their reference shelves.

Dictionary of Biblical Literacy. Compiled by Cecil B. Murphy, this book is subtitled *What Every Person Needs to Know*. And if you're trying to learn more about the vast and complex world embraced by the times, lands, and peoples of Scripture, this book is what is claims to be. I especially recommend the section "Life in Bible Times." Published by Oliver-Nelson Books (0-8407-9105-4).

Miscellaneous

Reader's Digest New Complete Do-It-Yourself Manual. This is a wonderful book, lavishly illustrated and coherently written. Whether you are a beginning fix-it person or an expert builder, this book will help you with everything from electrical wiring to mixing concrete to repairing furniture. "More to be desired than gold, yea, than much fine gold" (0-89577-378-3).

Flying by Foy. There is simply no group of people in all of show business who know more about creating the illusion of human beings flying through the air. Peter Foy and his family have been doing this since, well, as long as it's been done well and safely. Their services do not come cheap, and there are plenty of imitators who claim to do the same tricks for less money but who are really taking chances with the life of the actor to be flown. If you're certain you want to have flying angels in your Christmas show, contact Flying by Foy in Las Vegas at 702-454-3300.

Lee Shackleford. I would be glad to offer whatever advice or help I can with your effects or prop problem. (Although as with all the rest of the advice in this book, I can't offer any guarantees, warranties, or other liability!) Drop me a line at P.O. Box 547, Alabaster, AL 35007.

Glossary of Terms Used

Backstage: Literally "behind the scenes." Used to describe every area of the theatre that isn't onstage or in the audience.

Block, Blocking: The preplanned positions and movement of the actors, as designated by the director.

Business: A specific set of actions, usually without dialogue. A "sight gag" such as getting a pie in the face is a "piece of business." The soldiers nailing Jesus to the Cross are also "doing a piece of business."

Downstage: The part of the stage closest to the audience.

Flies, Fly Rails, Fly Space: The area directly over some large stages, equipped for hanging scenery that can be raised and lowered—which is called "flying."

Fresnel: pronounced freh-NEL, a kind of lighting instrument that uses a unique grooved lens to magnify and focus the light from its lamp.

Gloss: Reflective.

Gobo: A thin sheet of metal with a pattern punched through it. Correctly placed in a lighting instrument, it projects its pattern in sharp focus.

Grommet: A two-piece metal fastener, made of interlocking metal rings that can be hammered together, forming a tight-fitting "buttonhole" in heavy fabrics.

Lamp: In everyday household use, a *lamp* is an electrical device that holds a *bulb;* the lamp usually has a switch and it is the bulb that radiates light. In the theatre, more precise terminology is needed: the device that radiates the light is a *lamp* and the mechanism that holds it is an *instrument.*

Lighting Instrument: A special device built for the theatre, TV, and movies, emitting a tightly controlled beam of light.

Matte: Nonreflective.

Mime: To pretend to do something in such a way that you appear to be actually doing it. One example is drinking from an empty cup: if you do it so that another person cannot tell if the cup was empty or full, you have successfully mimed drinking.

Offstage: Anywhere that isn't onstage. See *Backstage.* Can also apply to the area on a stage that is immediately out of the audience's line-of-sight.

Papier-mâché: Pulpy compound that can be wetted, handled as if it were clay, then allowed to dry into a semirigid substance.

Palm: In an Easter pageant, you'd think this referred to the branches waved during the Triumphant Entry—but here we're talking about the sleight of hand method of concealing a small object in the palm of your hand. See Part Three of this book for a discussion of palming.

Pile: The fibers on a "furry" cloth that give it its texture.

Prosthetic, prosthesis: Literally, any artificial part added to a living being, such as an artificial leg or a glass eye. In "show business" the term usually refers specifically to false noses, pointed ears, and so on.

Revelation or *Reveal:* Not the vision of John the Divine, but the moment at which the audience first sees a character, set, prop, or whatever. Very often, intense dramatic moments depend on the way a character or item is *revealed*. See the discussion of the Ascension in this book for an example of how this affects the design of props and effects.

Scrim: A fabric often used in the theatre as a curtain or backdrop due to its ability to appear opaque or translucent, depending on how it is lit.

Slap-stick: Flat piece of wood or metal specially made for the purpose of creating a loud slapping noise.

Special: A lighting instrument set aside for a specific purpose.

Stage Blood: Syrupy mixture concocted to have the color and texture of human blood.

Stage Fog: Vaporized liquid simulating smoke, clouds, and fog when sprayed from a specialized machine.

Upstage: This theatre term has acquired two definitions. It refers to a stage's area furthest from the audience; and also to the habit some actors have of moving away from the audience while talking to another actor onstage, forcing the second actor to turn his back to the audience—thereby directing more attention at the actor who is doing the upstaging.

Index